Mindful Parenting

Finding Space To Be – In a World of To Do

Susan Bögels

T0288355

Mindful Parenting
Finding Space To Be – In a World of To Do

© Pavilion Publishing & Media Ltd

The author has asserted their rights in accordance with the Copyright, Designs and Patents Act (1988) to be identified as the author of this work.

Published by:
Pavilion Publishing and Media Ltd
Blue Sky Offices Shoreham
25 Cecil Pashley Way
Shoreham-by-Sea
West Sussex
BN43 5FF
Tel: 01273 434 943
Fax: 01273 227 308
Email: info@pavpub.com

Published 2020

A catalogue record for this book is available from the British Library.

ISBN: 978-1-912755-76-9

Pavilion Publishing and Media is a leading publisher of books, training materials and digital content in mental health, social care and allied fields. Pavilion and its imprints offer must-have knowledge and innovative learning solutions underpinned by sound research and professional values.

Editor: Ruth Chalmers, Pavilion Publishing and Media Ltd.
Cover design: Tony Pitt, Pavilion Publishing and Media Ltd.
Page layout and typesetting: Phil Morash, Pavilion Publishing and Media Ltd.
Translation: Leyla Perotti
Printing: CMP Digital Print Solutions

'*Showing you the world,
makes my life worth living.*'

Karl Ove Knausgård, Letter to an unborn daughter

Praise for *Mindful Parenting*

'At last, a book for parents by the world's leading expert in mindful parenting! Susan Bögels and her colleagues have spent over a decade figuring out precisely how and why mindfulness is so helpful to parents. She offers the reader her latest insights, along with charming personal examples and carefully selected practices that bring it all to life. This short book is packed with wisdom, candid and absolutely non-judgmental – a compelling road map for handling the trickiest dilemmas parenting has to offer.'

Christopher Germer, PhD
Faculty, Harvard Medical School
Author, The Mindful Path to Self-Compassion

'"I don't have time to do mindfulness - I've got kids". It is indeed the hardest thing to take time for yourself when you're juggling work, homemaking, and parenting. Any spare time you might have had has already been allocated. How on earth could you find time to meditate? Internationally acclaimed psychologist and mindfulness teacher Susan Bögels shows how this is possible. Yes, there are some short guided meditations to help you reclaim a few minutes of the day for yourself, but mostly she invites you to make your daily parenting schedule into your mindfulness curriculum. Sounds simple. It is. But remembering to do it is not so simple. So each week she suggests new methods that will help you. Research shows that cultivating these skills can help you transform your life: keeping your feet on the floor when things get tough, dissolving the over-critical voice in your head, and enriching your relationships with your children and wider family. I highly recommend this book.'

Mark Williams
Emeritus Professor of Clinical Psychology,
University of Oxford

'The most difficult task for a human being is being a parent. Mindful Parenting will be of assistance in this because it points to specific activities with well-specified aims, with an exceptionally well-structured training programme that will bring readers closer to being the best parent they can be. This scientifically grounded, well written, exceptionally accessible book should be required reading for all of us struggling to do the best we can with our sons and daughters. This book is highly recommended to anyone caring for children and young people.'

Peter Fonagy
Professor of Contemporary Psychoanalysis and Developmental Science,
University College London

Contents

About the author

Photograph by Kee & Kee

Susan Bögels is a Clinical Psychologist and Founder of the Mindful Parenting method. She is Professor of Family Mental Health, in particular focusing on the role of mindfulness, at the University of Amsterdam, and Founder of UvA Minds, an academic training and treatment centre for children and parents. She has published over 200 journal papers and is associate editor of the journal Mindfulness. She is lead author of the scholarly book *Mindful Parenting: A Guide for Mental Health Professionals* (Springer, 2014).

This book reflects two decades' experience of working with parents in mindful parenting courses and leading a research group exploring the role of attention in child development and psychopathology. It was also inspired by memories of Susan's own upbringing and of raising three children, and by her experiences as a participant and instructor in mindfulness retreats, training and personal meditation.

Foreword

Nirbhay N. Singh

Medical College of Georgia, Augusta University, Augusta, GA

As parents, particularly of young children or children with diverse abilities, we are constantly on the go. We are trapped in the doing mode because there is just so much to do! By the end of the day we feel we have not had a moment to catch our breath. Indeed, sometimes we feel so overwhelmed by the needs of our children that we slip into overdrive and respond on automatic pilot, occasionally wishing for what it could be rather than accepting what it is. This is not acceptance in the sense of passive resignation but, as Jon Kabat-Zin calls it *'radical acceptance'*. We can perceive the true nature of reality in those moments only by letting go of the thoughts that our mind produces. As Swami Vivekananda once said, *'We are what our thoughts have made us; so take care about what you think. Words are secondary. Thoughts live; they travel far'*. What if we could train our mind to let the thoughts pass without pulling them in, and inviting them to stay for coffee and cookies? Would this enable us to parent our children more mindfully? Can we teach our conceptual mind to function in a healthier manner such that we can be present for our children, mindful of our own needs as parents, and respond to both ourselves and our children with loving kindness and compassion?

All wisdom traditions have experientially perfected ways of teaching the mind to behave, thus enabling people to develop and embody mindfulness. Eastern concepts of mindfulness have trickled in over the last century, but it seeped into Western consciousness only over the last 50 years. The impetus for the spectacular growth of the field of mindfulness was Jon Kabat-Zinn's Mindfulness-Based Stress Reduction program aimed at using the wisdom of our own mind and body to face pain and suffering. Mindfulness meditation has entered the Western lexicon but the actual meaning of the term mindfulness has remained elusive, not only because something has been lost in the translation of the original Pali term *sati* (or *smṛti* in Sanskrit), but also because its meaning and practice is dependent on the spiritual lineage of modern meditation masters. Jon Kabat-Zinn has defined mindfulness as... *'the awareness that emerges through paying attention on purpose, in the present moment, and non-judgmentally to the unfolding of experience moment to moment'*. However, the great meditation master Munindra's view of mindfulness may work better in the context of mindful parenting, *'...experiencing from moment to moment, living from moment to moment, without clinging, without condemning, without judging, without criticizing—choiceless awareness… It should be integrated into our whole life. It is actually an education in how to see, how to hear, how to smell, how to eat, how to drink, how to walk with full awareness'*. When we are mindful, each moment, even in the chaos of daily parenting, may hold infinite possibilities.

What practicing mindfulness offers is nothing less than personal transformation in our daily life. What Susan Bögels offers in this book is a precise road map, a GPS to mindful parenting. She has distilled more than 20 years of experience in meditation and mindful parenting and produced a gem of a book that I wish I had when my wife and I were parenting our own children, but it is not too late for us to use with our grandchildren! There are many things I love about this book. First, it is written by an expert who not only has vast clinical experience but who also (and more importantly) has had to juggle an academic career, clinical work and consulting with raising her own children, all at the same time. So, she knows what parents go through when raising their children. Second, interspersed with the teachings throughout the book, you will find narratives of her own parenting practices, many of which you will be able to relate to on a personal level. She presents her struggles and successes with equal acceptance, encouraging you to validate and accept your parenting experiences with equanimity. Mindfulness is not a magic bullet for totally positive parenting but if you practice mindfulness with the right attitude and intention, and are mindfully present for your children, the outcomes for you and your children will be clearly evident. Third, she also details her own journey in the practice of meditation. She began as a novice but quickly mastered mindfulness meditation practices, used her personal discipline of meditation to sustain her daily life, and then engaged in developing and evaluating mindful parenting programs. Her earlier book, *Mindful Parenting: A guide for mental health practitioners*, was designed for professionals, but this book is for parents. No professional guidance is needed—just read a chapter and put the teachings into practice. Fourth, in this book Susan Bögels demonstrates a unique skill that most academics do not possess. Instead of turgid academic writing, she presents the book as a conversation with parents in unmistakably easy-to-read prose. She provides examples, describes what to do, how to do it, and then tells you what the mindfulness principle is called. She does this so casually that you may fail to appreciate how well she takes difficult mindfulness concepts and explains them in a way that my grandmother would understand without having any clarification questions.

This is a book that you want to learn from, cherish, and pass onto other parents. Its 11 chapters provide a range of specific mindfulness practices. Read each chapter at your own pace, immerse yourself in the practices, perform the easy-to-follow exercises, and transform your life, as well as those of your family and friends. The effects of your practices will cascade or spillover to everyone you come into contact with. Of course, reading this book alone will not get you far. Intellectual understanding of mindfulness meditation will arise as you read this book but, like all things, it will decay and pass away without practice of the teachings it presents.

Dhira – Self-Reliant

Look closely, my heart

See how all things
arise and pass way—

even that
which is turning
the shapes on this page
into the sounds
and thoughts
you are
right now
silently speaking
to yourself.

When you no longer need
to read the signs
to find your way,
you'll know for yourself
that books and maps
can only get you so far.

There is a direct path.

(Matt Weingast, *The First Free Women: Poems of The Early Buddhist Nuns*, 2020)

The direct path is mindfulness meditation. As meditation teachers emphasize: an ounce of practice is better than a ton of reading. Read this book and then practice, practice, practice.

Preface

I came to mindful parenting through a combination of my scientific and clinical work and my personal life. As a researcher I've studied the role of attention in problems such as social anxiety and blushing.[1,2,3] Whenever we feel tense or embarrassed in a social situation, perhaps because we're talking to someone we find attractive or admire professionally, we tend to see ourselves through the other person's eyes and worry what they'll think of us. In doing so we lose sight of the interaction and the moment, and end up stuck in stories about ourselves. If aspects of those stories are negative, this will only heighten our tension and shyness, for example by making us blush – which then makes us worry even more.

With my research group I developed a therapy called *task concentration training* (TCT). Using this, individuals with social anxiety and fear of blushing could learn to become aware of where their attention was focused in social situations, and to redirect it in more healthy ways. When our first paper on the positive effects of TCT was published in 1997[4], Professor Isaac Marks emailed me from the UK to ask: '*Isn't this the same as mindfulness?*'. I didn't know what mindfulness was and I certainly didn't want to appear stupid to a researcher whose work I much admired, so I studied the scientific literature of mindfulness. I was hooked – to the extent that I joined a Vipassana group and began my meditation practice.

I invited Professor Mark Williams, one of the leaders of the development of Mindfulness-Based Cognitive Therapy (MBCT) for depression[5], to provide mindfulness training to me and my colleagues. Staff from both the adult and child mental health care centres participated. At the adult centre we were already planning to research mindfulness for social anxiety[6], but after the training colleagues from the child centre were also interested in researching mindfulness. So in 2000 we ran a pilot study on mindfulness for young people with issues centred on attention difficulties, for example ADHD, autism and behaviour disorders. As most of these young people lived at home with their parents, it seemed important to give their parents parallel training in mindfulness principles, so we offered a course on 'mindful parenting'. This combined approach reduced the severity of the issues, and markedly improved the young people's attention control[7]. Parents reported great success against goals such as 'Being able to set limits to my child' and 'Sleep better', and many wished the training had been available sooner.

That's why we further developed mindful parenting as a standalone group training for parents. With Joke Hellemans I gave the first training in this form in 2008. The participants were parents who had been referred to our treatment centre because of problems with their child, problems that got in the way of healthy parenting, or problems in their relationship with their child. The children ranged from babies to adults (as one never stops being a parent).

In its first ten iterations, the group appeared effective in reducing parenting stress, improving parenting skills, and reducing problems like anxiety, depression, attention and behaviour problems in both parents and children.[8] Further research on ten more groups showed that the more parents improved in their mindful parenting, the more their children's symptoms reduced.[9] Next, we showed that the course was just as effective for parents and children who hadn't been referred to specialist mental health care[10], and finally we found that improvement in specific aspects of parenting correlated to improvements in specific types of issue in the child (e.g. anxiety, depression, attention problems).[11]

In 2014 I co-wrote a book presenting material from my mindful parenting course in a clinical and scientific way for mental health professionals.[12] The book you're now reading presents similar knowledge in an updated and much more accessible style for parents themselves and those who seek to guide and help them, and allows you to immerse yourself in the theory and practice of mindful parenting. It is the result of my experience teaching this approach for 20 years, and of the scientific knowledge produced by my own and others' research groups into the role of attention in children's development and well-being. It is also inspired by personal memories of how I myself was parented as a child, how I parented my own children, and my experiences in meditation and mindfulness during training events, shared retreats and at home on my meditation pillow.

Whether you're a parent, future parent, step-parent, foster parent, grandparent, caregiver or simply someone who wants to learn more about mindfulness and how it can be applied to parenting and other human relationships, I hope that you find value in this book. And when you reach the end, I hope the single most important insight you take away is that the relationship with your environment mirrors the relationship with your inner child. May your inner child benefit from this book as much as your loved ones and all the children in your life – past, present and future.

References

1 Bögels, S. M., Rijsemus, W., & De Jong, P. J. (2002). Self-focused attention and social anxiety: The effects of experimentally heightened self-awareness on fear, blushing, cognitions, and social skills. *Cognitive Therapy and Research*, **26**, 461-472.

2 Bögels, S. M., Alberts, M., & de Jong, P. J. (1996). Self-consciousness, self-focused attention, blushing propensity and fear of blushing. *Personality and Individual Differences*, **21**, 573-581.

3 Bögels, S. M., & Lamers, C. T. J. (2002). The causal role of self-awareness in blushing-anxious, socially-anxious and social phobics individuals. *Behaviour Research and Therapy*, **40**, 1367-1384.

4 Bögels, S. M., Mulkens, S., & De Jong, P. J. (1997). Practitioner task concentration report training and fear of blushing. *Clinical Psychology and Psychotherapy*, **4**, 251-258.

5 Segal, Z. V., Williams, J. M. G., & Teasdale, J. D. (2012). *Mindfulness-based cognitive therapy for depression*. New York: Guilford Press.

6 Bögels, S. M., Sijbers, G. F. V. M., & Voncken, M. (2006). Mindfulness and task concentration training for social phobia: A pilot study. *Journal of Cognitive Psychotherapy*, **20**, 33.

7 Bögels, S., Hoogstad, B., van Dun, L., de Schutter, S., & Restifo, K. (2008). Mindfulness training for adolescents with externalizing disorders and their parents. *Behavioural and Cognitive Psychotherapy*, **36**, 193-209.

8 Bögels, S. M., Hellemans, J., van Deursen, S., Römer, M., & van der Meulen, R. (2014). Mindful parenting in mental health care: effects on parental and child psychopathology, parental stress, parenting, coparenting, and marital functioning. *Mindfulness*, **5**, 536-551.

9 Meppelink, R., de Bruin, E. I., Wanders-Mulder, F. H., Vennik, C. J., & Bögels, S. M. (2016). Mindful parenting training in child psychiatric settings: heightened parental mindfulness reduces parents' and children's psychopathology. *Mindfulness*, **7**, 680-689.

10 Potharst, E. S., Baartmans, J.M.D., & Bögels, S.M. (2018). Mindful parenting in a clinical versus non-clinical setting: An explorative study. *Mindfulness*, 1-15.

11 Emerson, L. M., Aktar, E., de Bruin, E., Potharst, E., & Bögels, S. (2019). Mindful parenting in secondary child mental health: key parenting predictors of treatment effects. *Mindfulness*, 1-11.

12 Bögels, S., & Restifo, K. (2014). *Mindful parenting: A guide for mental health practitioners*. New York: Springer, Norton.

Introduction

I grew up during a period in the Netherlands when women were fired from jobs 'because of marriage'. Yet my mother had five children, worked full-time as an artist and fashion designer, and had a rich social life and many interests. When we came home from school each day, it wasn't our mother who welcomed us but a childminder. If anyone called for her, we'd ask them to call back after 6pm when she was home and cooking our dinner. The fact that our stories had to wait until Mum got home didn't bother me one bit as a child; I only wondered why she was always in a rush, and why the food was often not well cooked or burnt.

As a parent, I struggled and continue to struggle with the same double agenda – my passion for work and my wish to be with my children, physically and mentally. During part of my training as a psychotherapist I was pregnant with my first child. We were each asked to talk about our upbringings, and when it was my turn the other trainees asked '*Will you do it very differently from your Mum?*'. I was surprised because I wanted to be just like my Mum – juggling work, children and other interests. I wanted an intense life; or as John Kabat-Zinn, the founder of mindfulness in the Western world, calls it, '*full catastrophe living*'![1].

A few years later, with a young family and a budding career, I discovered meditation. Initially I meditated in the bath, so that I was still getting something done, or practiced yoga so that as well as meditating I was exercising. I found it very hard to take time for myself to do nothing but sit feeling my body, observing my mind, listening to the silence and being present in the moment. 'Not-doing' seemed much simpler in family life, where I could just be with my children, watching and listening to them and feeling wonder at their lives. At those times, there seemed to be no need to be anywhere other than where I was: with them.

Not for some time did it dawn on me that the hard work of sitting meditating on my pillow while there was so much to be done, and while there seemed to be so many more interesting things to focus on than myself, was making me far more aware of my parenthood, my children, and the precious time we had together.

So, what do we mean when we talk about mindful parenting?

Let's first look at what we mean by *parenting*. This means much more than superficially similar words like *rearing* and *raising*. All three require the provision of shelter and nourishment, but only parenting involves preparing someone physically and mentally for an independent life – and only parenting is indelibly associated with effort and worry. Forming and developing our children to be helpful members of society causes us stress, specifically *parenting stress*.

Parenting stress springs from questions in parents' minds (*'Will my child turn out well?' 'Will she get a good job?' 'Will he be happy?'*), tasks that parents must fulfil as part of and alongside their parenting, and a host of other possible factors. It can narrow our perspective, destroy the pleasure of parenting and turn us into impulsive, unpredictable, frightening beings. Parenting stress shapes the family environment, and it can begin to affect a child even when it is still in the womb.[2]

So, now that we have considered parenting in general, what is mindful parenting?

Jon Kabat-Zinn defines *mindfulness* as *'directing the attention in a special way: intentionally, in the present moment, and without judgment'*. He developed Mindfulness-Based Stress Reduction (MBSR) training[1], an approach that helped people to reduce their stress substantially in a short time, and improve their quality of life. In 1998 he and his wife Mila published their book *Everyday Blessings: The inner work of mindful parenting*, which to my knowledge is the first time the term 'mindful parenting' was ever used.[2] When Kathleen Restifo and I wrote our 2014 book *Mindful Parenting: A guide for mental health practitioners*[3], Jon and Mila developed a new definition of mindful parenting just for us:

> *'Mindful parenting is an ongoing creative process, not an end point. It involves intentionally bringing non-judgmental awareness, as best we can, to each moment. This includes being aware of the inner landscape of our own thoughts, emotions and body sensations, and the outer landscape of our children, our family, our home, and the broader culture we inhabit. It is an on-going practice that can grow to include (1) greater awareness of a child's unique nature, feelings and needs; (2) a greater ability to be present and listen with full attention; (3) recognizing and accepting things as they are in each moment, whether pleasant or unpleasant; (4) recognizing one's own reactive impulses and learning to respond more appropriately and imaginatively, with greater clarity and kindness.'*[4]

This book consists of 11 chapters about facets of mindful parenting as defined by Jon and Mila. I suggest that you approach it as a self-help course, reading one chapter per week and doing the associated exercises, but of course it's up to you. However you choose to use it, please don't make the mistake (as I did, initially) of thinking that reading about mindfulness is the same as practicing it. Only through putting the principles of mindfulness and meditation into practice for yourself will the knowledge become embedded and 'stick'. Personal experience is essential, so don't just think about mindful parenting – try it out! Read each chapter mindfully, with deliberate, non-judgmental, here-and-now attention, and don't rush to get to the end. The reading takes as long as it takes.

Each chapter ends with a series of practices to do that week (and, if mindfulness grabs you as it did me, for the rest of your life). Some have accompanying audio tracks, which as a buyer of this book you can download from www.pavpub.com/mindful-parenting-resources. Often when presenting these exercises I'll suggest that you record your experiences in your notebook. This can be a real notebook or a computer, but I do recommend that you do keep a journal of some sort – over time it will become a unique account of your experiences and progress in mindfulness that you can revisit whenever you need it again.

Above all, let go of any and all expectations about what you might get from the practices – you don't need to enjoy a practice or achieve a tangible result for it to be an important and helpful step on your journey. With mindful parenting, as with parenting more generally, the experience itself is what really counts.

References

1   Kabat-Zinn, J. (2013). *Full catastrophe living, revised edition: How to cope with stress, pain and illness using mindfulness meditation*. London: Hachette UK.

2   Kabat-Zinn, M. & Kabat-Zinn, J. (1998; 2014) *Everyday blessings: The inner work of mindful parenting*. London: Hachette UK.

3   Bögels, S., & Restifo, K. (2014). *Mindful Parenting: A guide for mental health practitioners*. New York: Springer, Norton.

4   Kabat-Zinn, M. & Kabat-Zinn, J. (2012). Personal communication.

Chapter 1:
Mindful parenting: Being there without prejudice or judgement

'Nothing will stay with us if we don't give it our full attention.'

Of all our unpaid tasks, parenting is the one that the majority of us devote most time and attention to (or feel we do, anyway). It's also the one that worries us most when it doesn't go well, and the one we talk about most. Research shows that the amount of time we spend with our children is increasing, for both parents. In 1965 mothers spent a weekly average of 10.5 hours with their children, and fathers 2.6 hours. By 2010 the

average had risen to 13.7 hours for mothers and 7.2 hours for fathers[1]. This still isn't much, by the way: two hours a day for mothers and one for fathers, spread across all their children. Yet during the same period, the time spent by mothers in paid employment has risen dramatically and fathers' working hours haven't gone down. So the question is – where have parents found those extra hours?

Time is a necessary condition for attention, but it isn't sufficient in itself. A question that parents are never asked in this kind of research is how many minutes of the daily time spent with their children is their attention truly focused on the children? Picture it: your child comes home from school and you ask how their day was, and in the course of an enthusiastic but rather long answer your mind wanders to other things. You think of emails you need to answer, shopping you need to do, your other child who needs to be picked from a club soon. You nod, smile, and perhaps even respond to what your child is saying (*'That's great, well done!'*) but you haven't really followed what made their day so special and you can't really share in their happiness because you weren't paying full attention. If you're lucky your child will catch you out: *'You're not really listening! I already told you that… didn't you hear me?'*.

Lienhard Valentin, a passionate author and publisher of books about mindfulness and parenting[2], invited me to give a course on mindful parenting in Germany. While I was there, he showed me a video of an orphanage in Hungary where young babies who had been abandoned by their parents were raised by carers trained to look after children in a mindful way[3]. The time the carers have for each child is no more than in other orphanages. But when they change a baby's nappy, for example, they have been trained to keep their attention fully focused on that baby, ignoring the other babies and their crying.

We watched an interaction between a carer and a baby with serious developmental problems relating to premature birth and trauma. Difficult to wake, the baby was largely unresponsive, giving few indications of what she did or didn't want. The carer came across as highly 'centred': her actions were calm, loving and attentive, based on a deep trust in herself and in this fragile, vulnerable, and entirely dependent little human being entrusted to her care. She announced all her actions through verbal and non-verbal signals, and you could almost feel the back of her hand stroking the baby's cheek. She looked at and listened to the baby with undivided attention, reacting to all her signals, however tiny. She completely ignored the ceaseless crying of other babies, appearing to be fully absorbed in this particular moment with this particular child.

We then saw the same carer dress a slightly older boy with the same undivided, unconditional and loving attention, once again entirely absorbed in this specific moment with this particular child. She responded attentively to all the boy's behaviours, even if they were unrelated to dressing. As a result, the process of getting dressed took as long as he needed it to, because this was his time with the carer. She offered him a choice of two sweaters, once again giving him space, and followed him in the process of choosing – how he pointed at one then the other, making a game of it. Watching, I felt no impatience whatsoever; time seemed to stand still in this moment in which carer and child shared the experience of dressing. You could feel the carer's trust that, through their interaction and joint attentiveness to the moment, the child would eventually end up dressed – as would all the others after him.

As I watched, I sensed a deep calm and silence, despite the noise of other children crying in the background. They had to wait; but each of them knew that they would also get their moment in which the carer would give them her undivided attention, and so they soothed themselves. These short but fully attentive interactions allowed the children to heal their traumas.

Children get to know themselves through the attention their parents and other carers pay to them, which is also known as 'mirroring'[4]. Parents mimic the facial expressions of their infants without even realizing it. They read the facial expressions of their child very carefully and follow their movements and sounds attentively, trying to understand what their baby wants. This attention that parents (and other professional carers) pay to a developing child is as vital to its survival as food and oxygen. Through it, the infant learns to experience itself as an integrated whole. It learns to feel its centre, its self, the point from which its interactions with the outside world emerge, and to which it can return when it is saturated with new impressions or when others have no time for it (as in the case of the babies in the orphanage). So when speaking about being 'centred' here, I am referring to an attitude that we can cultivate through meditation, and one that children learn through attentive interaction with their parents and carers.

Children try to draw their parents' attention to things they notice by pointing or, if they can talk, saying, *'look!'*, *'listen!'*, *'feel!'*, *'taste!'* This is a process we call *joint attention*, and it is an important indicator of healthy development – it has been found that children suffering from autism, depression and/or neglect develop this kind of behaviour later and to a lesser degree[5]. When parents and children pay joint attention to something, it helps the child to concentrate. After all, if a parent is truly focused on something, then it tells the child that it must be important – and so, with the parent's encouragement, the child keeps looking more closely, for longer or more often. When parents do not engage in much mirroring behaviour, i.e. they pay little attention to what the child feels, says and does, and fail to look or only superficially looks at what the child points out, it can have the opposite effect. The child may not develop a sense of self, or experience himself or herself as a whole to the same degree. The child may be less centred, and may pay less frequent, shorter and more superficial attention to things.

Compared to other species, human children take longest to reach the point where they can survive without the care of their parents. This is related to the size of a baby's skull, which in turn is a result of our large brains – particularly our frontal lobes, a feature that distinguishes us from other animals. To grow such a large skull, the baby must be born very early in developmental terms, long before it can walk, feed and protect itself. That's why it takes a huge amount of effort to raise a human child. We are evolved parents[6]: the way we raise children has been shaped by natural selection, because tactics that increased the chances of a child reaching adulthood were more likely to be passed on to the next generation. In the history of our evolution, the fact that a mother had to feed her baby so often and for so long at the start of its life made the mother and child vulnerable to outside attack, and dependent on the father, grandparents, siblings and wider community for protection and food. This is why people raised their children in groups, and where the expression 'It takes a village to raise a child' comes from.

Very little is left of this communal way of bringing up children in contemporary society. We tend to live in nuclear rather than communal family units, and in cities in particular there is little social cohesion and control. Rather than being looked after by grandparents, other family members, friends or neighbours while their parents work, children tend to be looked after by day care professionals or paid childminders.

Because caring for children involves so many things, it risks becoming one long list of to-dos. It is all too easy to crunch through tasks without giving any of them our full attention. Operating in this way is sometimes referred to as the *doing mode*[7] – a state of mind in which we get things done, solve problems and tick off jobs, and are aware of what is done and what still needs doing. The doing mode lets us efficiently carry out tasks we're familiar with, and which don't require much conscious awareness on our part – such as feeding the children, cleaning the house and traveling to work. In the doing mode we're generally on autopilot, so to speak – it's our default mode. Often our thoughts are ahead of us – while driving to work you may be thinking about the day ahead, for example, or while taking your children to school you may be thinking about who will collect them. The doing mode is drilled into children from a young age, both by parents and at school: '*Hurry up or you'll be late! If you finish your homework you can have an ice cream. Stop dawdling!*'.

There is another mode, however, that every human being is also born with, and that is the *being mode*[7]. In the being mode we are connected to the present, we can experience things at this particular moment in time, and we can let things be just how they are. We're accepting and open to pleasant, neutral and unpleasant feelings (our own and those of others), we don't try to change any aspect of our experience, and we feel calm, still and centred. By nature, children are in the being mode. Walking to school, they don't think about the time or their destination; instead they stop to look at flowers or jump in puddles – they are focused on the present moment in the present place.

Since I learned about these two states of mind I've developed a habit: whenever I write yet another to-do list on a yellow sticky note, I also write a 'to-be list' on a pink or blue note to remind myself what life's really about. Don't get me wrong – ticking off to-do lists performs a valuable function by getting things done and activating a reward centre in the brain. Each time you tick off a task, you automatically reward yourself: well done! But what's important is to find a balance between the doing and being modes in the manner in which we carry out tasks and attempt to achieve our goals.

To do:
- buy Jack a birthday present
- take Eva to swimming
- call school about lost homework
- ask Lucy to stay over with Anna
- help Lucy pack her bag
- bake cupcakes for school with Jack

To be:
- calm
- attentive
- patient
- in contact/together
- enjoying the moment

Parenting seems itself to have become an item on life's to-do list, something we feel obliged to succeed at – with success defined in terms of characteristics like beauty, education, achievement and social skills. We compare our own children to those of others who seem to be doing better on those fronts. We're influenced by magazines showing pictures of happy families eating together during the Christmas holidays – everyone smiling, beautiful and slim, with perfect hair and makeup, in a bright tidy house with wonderful looking food laid out on a perfectly decorated table.

Thinking back to Christmas meals in my family when I was growing up, memories of a different kind come to mind. The turkey that was undercooked because it was put in the oven too late. My father pulling a melted plastic bag with giblets out of the bird when it was finally put on the table – which was *not* seen as a laughing matter. The children arguing or giggling, resulting in our father sending all five of us upstairs one by one, without our dinner, leaving my parents alone at the Christmas table – and deeply unhappy, I imagine. No doubt they had their own expectations of what a Christmas meal should look like – how festive the atmosphere should be, what the turkey should taste like and whose responsibility that was, and how the children should behave.

During the holidays my parents were clearly in a doing mode, experiencing a gap between the way things ought to be and the way they actually were. As a child, I remember feeling the tension and fear of things going wrong – and the loneliness when they did, again. But what might have happened if my parents had taken a mindful parenting course and learned about the being mode? Could they have looked at their table of bickering children, the underdone turkey with its melted plastic interior, their unfulfilled expectations about each other and their own shortcomings, and given up trying to turn the experience it into something other than it actually was? What might have happened if my mother had cooked the turkey with real attention, and been aware of what she needed from her husband and children in order to do so? Or if my father had looked at my mother with real, open attention, and seen that she would have much preferred to be painting rather than cooking – that she was so worn out from caring for five children, in addition to a more than full-time job and a busy social life, that he could have given her no greater pleasure than by putting the turkey in the oven himself?

I have much happier memories of Easter and how our mother would decorate eggs with us according to a custom passed down from my Polish great-grandmother. I remember the smell of melting wax, from the crayons we used to draw on the warm, round surface of the eggs, and how we'd dunk the eggs into different coloured paint baths, delighted at the white lines that appeared where we'd applied the wax. Then the smell of the vinegar bath, and finally of the butter we used to polish the eggs until they shone. I still follow this same custom for decorating eggs every Easter, as do my own children.

In parenting and in family life, the being mode means seeing our children, our partners and ourselves the way they and we really are, without trying to change anything. A simple way to practice this is with the weather. When we leave home each morning we have no control over the weather outside. Instead of trying to resist the prevailing conditions (e.g. head down and shoulders hunched when it's raining, windy or cold) we can cultivate an attitude of openness and acceptance of this particular weather on this particular day. How does it feel – the rain on your face, the wind whistling past your head, the cold against your skin? We can experience the weather just the way it is at that particular moment, letting go completely of any idea that it should be different.

I get the perfect chance to practice this attitude when I spend camping holidays on an island off the north coast of the Netherlands. After days of bad weather, I always hear parents in the shower block telling their children, 'Next year we'll go to the south of France!'. They are no longer in the moment, on the present holiday, but planning another one which should be better. Children don't think this way: they experience the weather just the way it is, at that moment, and play in the shower block when it's too wet outside and too cold in the tent. We adults could learn something from that!

Cognitive psychologists conduct a good deal of research into biases, which are prejudices or distortions of reality[8]. Our minds work in such a way that biases maintain themselves. Once we get a certain idea about how reality is (e.g. *I can't write*), we pay selective attention to events or information that seem to confirm this idea (*the bad mark I got for that essay*), while ignoring other information that doesn't confirm it or even contradicts it (*that grade was due to poor spelling*; *I was asked to write for the school magazine*). We fix our identities in this way, depriving ourselves of space to develop. And we don't just do it to ourselves; unintentionally, we also do it to our children.

Visiting Professor Alan Stein's lab in Oxford, I watched footage of mothers with eating disorders spoon-feeding their babies their first solids. These mothers were worried that the babies would get dirty, or become overweight. What should have been a celebratory and playful moment, in which mother and child jointly discover solid food, was a stressful experience for them. They held certain biases (e.g. *eating makes you fat*), which they projected onto their babies. And it isn't only mothers with eating disorders who have problematic biases; parents with social anxiety disorders, who are afraid of being negatively evaluated by others[9], tend to worry that their babies will also be judged negatively, and parents who suffer from depression or borderline personality disorder think their children don't like them and ignore the smiles their baby sends their way. In the worst cases, a mother with severe postnatal depression may go so far as to kill herself because she is convinced that her baby is better off without her.

Psychological disorders can be the seeds of bias. However, the ways in which parents who do not suffer from psychological disorders view their children is also coloured by all kinds of biases, both positive and negative, which can hinder a child's development. Parents who give a child positive labels such as 'athletic', 'gifted' or 'responsible' can unwittingly limit that child's development. For example, a 'responsible' child is often put in charge of their brothers and sisters, depriving them of opportunities to develop their own playful side. The 'athletic' child is constantly training, and never learns simply to relax and do nothing. And the 'gifted' child, while challenged intellectually, isn't invited to discover the more earthly pleasures of working with their hands.

These kinds of positive biases can also lead parents and other caregivers to miss signals that a child needs their help, and to have problems accepting any behaviour that does not conform to the child's 'label'. I remember how my daughter, who scored highly on cognitive tests, came home disappointed after giving her first school presentation, which was about whales. *I expected more from you*, is what her teacher had said.

The label 'intelligent' had inadvertently blinded the teacher (and me) to the difficulty my daughter had with structuring information in the orderly way required for a presentation.

Positive labels can also have a negative effect on a child's sibling: the brother or sister of a responsible, athletic or gifted child can be perceived as irresponsible, unathletic or slow, and develop accordingly. I remember how my teachers used to sigh and say, '*You're not like your sister*' (who was more serious, hardworking, and organized than me and got better grades), and how I did my best to conform to that negative image by doing as little work as possible and getting the lowest possible pass grades.

Any diagnostic labels a child may be given, such as ADHD, autism, sensitivity or fear of failure, can also serve as biases that limit parents in paying attention to their child in a truly open way. One mother told me how, after a healthcare professional had called her son autistic, she began to experience her son's habit of arranging his soft toys in order of size, in a completely different way. Behaviour that she'd previously seen as attentive, precise and endearing, she now viewed as rigid and childish, triggering feelings of fear and aversion.

Because we spend so much time with our children, we develop all kinds of interactions that become habitual. These habitual patterns lead us to react in the same ways we've always done, and can limit a child's development. Researcher Jean Dumas carried out an elegant experiment in which he asked teachers to categorize pupils as either socially competent, average, aggressive or anxious[10]. Each group consisted of 30 children with an average age of four. The children's mothers were asked to perform a task once with their own child and once with someone else's child, without taking control. The task was to push a toy trolley around a miniature supermarket and gather five items on a list from shelves containing different categories of products, taking the shortest possible route for each item on the list. The interactions between the mothers and children were filmed and assessed by psychologists trained to score parental behaviour in terms of 'positivity' and 'reciprocity'. The observers did not know which child was the mother's own.

The study found that the mothers of aggressive and anxious children scored lower in terms of positivity and reciprocity when reacting to their own children than mothers with average or competent children. However, the same mothers displayed equal levels of both qualities when interacting with other children. This shows that the mothers of aggressive and anxious children are capable of reacting just as positively and reciprocally as the mothers of average and competent children, and the way they interact with their own child has developed over time rather than being 'inbuilt'.

The way parents see their child can be affected by all kinds of biases or distortions, resulting from their own or the child's problems, diagnostic labels, comparisons between children and interactions developed over time. Parents can also hold biases resulting from the way they were themselves brought up. If their own parents were critical and disapproving, then they may have internalized this behaviour and adopt a similar attitude to their own children. Wherever parental biases come from, they have the potential to hinder a child's development and disrupt a healthy parent-child relationship.

So how can we lessen the effects of such biases to give our children the best chance to develop in a balanced way, based on their own talents and ambitions? One thing parents can practice is approaching their child with a *beginner's mind*, which means looking at them as if they're seeing them for the first time. Doing things with a beginner's mind means doing them with full and open attention. Use all your senses, as this helps to absorb you in the experience. Think back to when your child was just born: do you remember the smells, the sounds, the way they looked and moved, how they felt? Did you feel a sense of wonder, surprise or curiosity? Can you recall how you held your baby for the first time? That's the beginner's mind.

A good technique for seeing your child with a beginner's mind is to try to see them not as 'your child' but as 'a child'. Here's an example to illustrate how this works: what would you think if your son threw himself onto the floor screaming at the supermarket checkout because he couldn't have the chocolate bar he wanted? Perhaps you'd think he was spoiled, that it was your fault, or that you were a bad parent? Now, what if it was someone else's child having such a tantrum? Does your response change to thinking that children must learn that they can't always get what they want, that the parent is right not to give in, or that chocolate shouldn't be displayed at supermarket checkouts?!

Looking at your son or daughter as 'a child' instead of 'your child' is the first beginner's mind exercise we give to parents on our mindful parenting courses, and it can have a powerful and liberating effect. One mother talked about using a beginner's mind to observe her son while he was reading. He had been diagnosed with ADHD, and she was often irritated by his loud and fidgety behaviour, including when he was reading. She tended not to look at or listen to him in such moments. Now, as she observed her child as if for the first time, she noticed not just his beautiful hair and fine features, but also how much enjoyment he got from reading. He empathized with the story, laughing, frowning, cheering, looking surprised and moving about enthusiastically while immersed in the story. Now, instead of being irritated, she enjoyed watching her child enjoy himself.

Exercises

Exercise 1.1: Sitting meditation (audio track 1)

This is a ten-minute sitting meditation, in which you focus awareness on your breathing. Find a quiet spot where you feel relaxed and safe, and where you won't be disturbed. You can meditate sitting on a chair, cushion or meditation bench. Make sure you're warm – put a blanket around you if you need to, and wear socks – and sitting comfortably. It's best if you can do the meditation once a day for a week. If you find you reach a point where you know the audio track by heart, you can do it unguided and set an alarm to go off after ten minutes (or however long you want to meditate). Let go of any expectations about what you should be experiencing – just doing it is all that matters. Afterwards, make notes about your first experiences of meditation in your notebook if you wish.

Exercise 1.2: Beginner's-mind parenting

Choose five minutes this week to observe your child as unobtrusively as possible. You can do it while they're sleeping, playing, reading, sitting at the computer, watching TV or any other situation that seems suitable. Open up all your senses and observe your child as fully as you can, as if you're seeing this child for the first time. You can also imagine that you're a painter, illustrator, reporter, photographer or video artist. What does the child look like? Observe colours, shapes, light and dark. Notice all the little details, zooming in and out, from details to the bigger picture and back. Carefully observe the way they move. Listen to the different sounds: the tone of their voice, noises they make when moving, the sound of their breathing perhaps, or the beating of their heart. You can also use your other senses, depending on the situation. If you're sitting close to your child, you may be able to pick up the smell of their skin, body, hair or clothing. Can you feel anything? Maybe your child is leaning against you or sitting on your lap. Can you taste anything, for example if your young child sticks a finger in your mouth? What does it feel like to watch your child like this, with a beginner's mind, like you're seeing them for the first time? Don't try to change the experience in any way; it is what it is. Make notes about your experience in your notebook if you wish.

Exercise 1.3: Bringing full attention to a routine action with or for your child

Routine actions are things we do automatically (at least in part), because they don't require much attention: they have become habitual. This allows us to do them while doing something else at the same time, like peeling potatoes while we watch TV or driving while our thoughts wander. This week, pick a routine action, one that you do with or for your child at least once a day, and carry it out with full attention as if you're doing it for the first time. It could be taking them to school, asking how their day was, dressing them, brushing their teeth, preparing their lunch, serving their dinner, or saying goodnight. Make sure the action doesn't take up too much time. If you want to choose something that takes longer, use just the first few minutes for the exercise.

Focus your attention on your child, on yourself, and on the contact between you. Let the experience be the way it is. The only objective is to be aware of this moment, just as it is. To observe a routine action consciously, it can help to slow it down a bit. Once you've decided which routine action with or for your child you want to carry out with your full attention, keep it up for a week. Don't switch between different actions. Make notes about your experiences in your notebook if you wish.

Exercise 1.4: Joint attention

Watch out for moments when your child asks you to pay joint attention to something: *'Daddy, Mummy, look!'*, *'Listen to this song'*, *'Look at this video'*, *'Guess what I got for my test?'*. What kinds of things does your child want to look at with you? When you look at something with your child, try to give it your full and undivided attention, and do this for longer, more deeply or more often than you would usually do. Make notes if you wish.

References

1   Bianchi, S.M. (2000). Maternal employment and time with children: Dramatic change or surprising continuity? *Demography*, **37**, 401-414.

2   Valentin, L., & Kunze, P. (2010). *Die Kunst, gelassen zu erziehen: Buddhistische Weisheit für den Familienalltag*. Munchen: Gräfe und Unzer.

3   Eisi4 (2009). *Pflege I-1: LOCZY – Wo kleine Menschen groß werden*. Available at: https://www.youtube.com/watch?v=AG7MUM_d32I (accessed January 2020).

4   Fonagy, P., Gergely, G., & Jurist, E. L. (Eds.). (2004). *Affect regulation, mentalization and the development of the self*. London: Karnac books.

5   Frith, U. (1991). Asperger and his syndrome. *Autism and Asperger syndrome*, **14**, 1-36.

6   Bögels, S. M., & Restifo, K. (2014). *Mindful parenting: A guide for mental health practitioners*. Chapter 2: Evolutionary perspectives on parenting and parenting stress. New York: Springer.

7   Segal, Z. V., Williams, J. M. G., & Teasdale, J. D. (2012). *Mindfulness-based cognitive therapy for depression*. New York: Guilford Press.

8   Beck, A. T. (Ed.). (1979). *Cognitive therapy of depression*. New York: Guilford Press.

9   de Vente, W., Majdandzic, M., Colonnesi, C., & Bögels, S. M. (2011). Intergenerational transmission of social anxiety: the role of paternal and maternal fear of negative child evaluation and parenting behaviour. *Journal of Experimental Psychopathology*, **2**, 509-530.

10 Dumas, J. E., & LaFreniere, P. J. (1993). Mother-child relationships as sources of support or stress: A comparison of competent, average, aggressive, and anxious dyads. *Child Development*, **64**, 1732-1754.

Chapter 2:
Being your own parent:
Self-care and compassion

'If you do not know how to take care of yourself, and the violence in you, then you will not be able to take care of others. You must have love and patience before you can truly listen to your partner or child. If you are irritated you cannot listen. You have to know how to breathe mindfully, embrace your irritation and transform it.'
Thich Nhat Hanh[1]

On an aircraft, the safety instruction is always to put on your own oxygen mask before fitting your child's. Parents need reminding of this, because nowhere else do we show such extraordinary altruism as where our children are concerned. Parents of young children eat standing up or forget to use the bathroom, so involved are they with their offspring. Parents of older children stay awake half the night because their adolescent hasn't yet returned, or spend hours helping with homework before even thinking about tasks they need to do for themselves.

By taking such good care of our children, we risk exhausting ourselves physically and emotionally. Self-care and self-compassion are antidotes to this exhaustion. If in our own childhood we experienced parents who were not sufficiently present or dependable, then practicing self-care and self-compassion becomes even more important because we haven't learned by example how to look after others while also looking after ourselves. Worse, the moments when we are most in need of self-care – such as when facing difficult events like illness, relationship issues or aging parents – are exactly those moments when we often forget it.

This chapter is about paying attention to ourselves and our bodies, and how self-care and self-compassion can help us to manage the stresses of parenting. When I run mindful parenting training groups, we always discuss the extent to which parents succeed in taking a 'breathing space' in moments of parental stress. A breathing space is a three-minute meditation practice in which we stop everything we're doing in order to notice our breath and pay attention to how we are right now. I remember clearly one mother telling me in an outraged tone: *'But I don't have time in my busy life for three minutes of breathing space!'*.

In fact, three minutes is less time than smokers take for themselves each time they light a cigarette. Yet I can understand that mother's concern. Whenever I attend a residential silent retreat, which I allow or force myself to do once a year, I feel guilty toward my children because I'm leaving them in the care of others. I feel guilty toward my children's babysitters or their friends' parents, and I feel guilty toward my colleagues. All are taking on extra work so I can do nothing!

But of course, I don't do nothing. When I meditate for a week I practice *not doing*, and that is a huge job. At the start of the retreat, the meditation teacher usually opens by explaining how our attendance is a gift to our children, partners and colleagues, and the world. Meditation teacher Edel Maex once told me how happy his wife is whenever he goes on retreat, because it makes him a better person. By taking care of ourselves, we are also caring for those around us.

Caring for ourselves starts with being aware of what's going on inside us, of how we are. Only when we're aware can we begin to look after our own needs. We humans are equipped with a remarkable ability to repress needs and feelings when they don't serve us. We can 'postpone' illness until after a big deadline, thanks to the adrenaline and dopamine hormones that we produce when we're busy with important things, and when faced with danger we can bypass hunger, thirst or fatigue so as to concentrate our reserves for a 'fight-or-flight' action.

We have also evolved to put our children first in times of need or threat. Now, it is remarkable enough that we do this in life-or-death situations; that we also do it without thinking in less perilous circumstances is nothing short of astonishing. As an aunt once told me, *'I have taught my children everything, except to take account of me'*. By taking care of ourselves, we also teach our children to take us into account.

I remember how, just after my divorce, I missed my children terribly when they were with their father and I made sure I was 100% available for them when they were with me. All weekend I would dedicate myself to them. However, doing this meant skipping my Saturday morning hour alone on the couch with a cappuccino and a newspaper, and every Monday I went back to work happy but exhausted.

At my children's school I noticed that a very capable teacher sometimes hung up a sign saying 'DO NOT DISTURB'. When this sign was up the children weren't allowed to ask the teacher questions, but instead had to find their own solutions and help each other while the teacher focused on a few children with special needs.

I decided to introduce 'DO NOT DISTURB' time at home. My children cooperated enthusiastically – they answered the phone during my reinstated Saturday hour, and told callers that their mother was unavailable because she was reading the newspaper and drinking coffee! My son helped his younger sister go to the toilet, and when she ran around with scissors he took them from her. In his very first diary, which he showed me, he wrote about my hour for myself, which clearly had a special meaning for him. So, without doubt, I not only did myself a favour but also gave my children something important in their own young lives.

Caring for ourselves requires that now and then we distance ourselves from what meditation teacher Edel Maex calls so beautifully *'the maelstrom of life'*[2], and instead take time to notice how we are and what we might need. Self-care starts with listening to our body. When we take a step back, drop into our body and fully experience sensations, we tune in to ourselves – which is the first step in tuning in to our children.[3] How can we expect to understand, communicate with and relate to our offspring if we have lost contact with ourselves?

We tend to ignore our body when we're busy with work, children, or the home – because feelings of tiredness, pain or stress aren't helpful at such times. We can also lose touch with pleasant physical sensations. Can you remember how it felt to walk with your child on your shoulders and tiny hands in your hair? By connecting with our body we can reconnect with special moments like these, and in the process step out of the 'doing mode'.

What do you feel in your body when you eat, read a newspaper, shower, bake a cake, travel to work or pick up the children from school? Being aware of our physical state is the first step in taking care of ourselves. Caring for our body begins with simple, concrete things like eating or drinking when we notice hunger or thirst, stopping when we notice we are full or no longer thirsty, going to the toilet when we notice the urge, sleeping when we notice tiredness, moving when we notice stiffness, walking when we notice restlessness and so on.

Being present with our body and taking care of it can also be practiced when we're in contact with our child. How do we stand when we bathe our baby, how do we sit when we feed our toddler, what happens in our body when we start a difficult conversation with our adolescent? We can learn to listen to the life in our body and the wisdom of it. The 'body scan' is a formal meditation in which we scan our entire body, and cultivate bodily awareness, and as such it is a cornerstone of mindfulness and of this book. Yet this same bodily awareness can also be achieved by simply walking, cycling, swimming or playing sports, if we take time to pay attention to how the body feels during and after the activity.

Self-compassion is a way to take care of ourselves, and it is especially important in moments of stress, suffering, (self-) criticism, (self-) judgment, or failure. To understand self-compassion, it is important first to know what is meant by compassion in general. One way to define compassion is *'suffering with someone'*. Researcher and compassion teacher Kristin Neff[4] describes compassion as follows:

> *'Compassion presupposes the recognition and clear seeing of suffering. It entails feelings of kindness, care, and understanding for people who are in pain, so that the desire to ameliorate suffering naturally emerges. Finally, compassion involves recognizing the shared human condition, fragile and imperfect as it is. Self-compassion has exactly the same qualities – it's just compassion turned inward.'*

Compassion is something we all naturally have in us. I know I do. As a child I was always saving animals, volunteering in charity shops, raising money for starving children in Africa (with great shame I must confess that I once spent collected money on two terrapins, and when they died I saw it as divine punishment), and worrying about global pollution and the suffering of living creatures. My school speeches were about my heroes Gandhi and Martin Luther King, who showed compassion for their people by suffering with them. I read all the books I could find about the Holocaust, and tried to imagine the suffering of the Jewish people. In my adolescence, I cried about the fate of favourite music stars like Jimi Hendrix, and read books by and about people who had committed suicide[5] like writer Sylvia Plath, mourning the loss of these unique talents. And I watched movies like *One Flew Over the Cuckoo's Nest* and wanted to end abuse in psychiatry. Becoming a psychotherapist was my calling. From the start, I wanted to ease the suffering of others. That I also hoped ultimately to alleviate my own suffering and heal my own traumas, I did not know at that early stage.

Compassion, then, is a tendency to place ourselves in the shoes of others who suffer, and to try to help. We experience compassion naturally for our children: many parents say they didn't know they could love someone so much until they had a child. Of course, we don't always feel this way. Sometimes we can show strong negative emotions and behaviour towards our children (about which more later), but the point is that when as parents we connect to the boundless love we can feel for our children, we become aware of our own innate capacity to love a child and take care of it – and to do the same for ourselves.

Researchers Caroline Falconer, Mel Slater and others have used virtual reality techniques to investigate the effects of self-compassion on people suffering from a depressive disorder, and they have made a video of their experiment publicly available[6]. We know that depressed people can be extremely self-critical, isolate themselves from others and tend not to be self-compassionate when they have difficulties.

In a virtual reality environment (called a 'cave') the researchers asked their subjects to comfort a virtual child who was upset. They were told to say in a kind voice the following sentences to the child:

> *'It's not nice when things happen to us that we don't like. It's really upset you, hasn't it? You know, sometimes when we're sad, it's really helpful to think of someone who loves us and is kind to us. Can you do that for me, can you think of someone who loves you and is kind to you? What might they say to you now that would make you feel a bit better?'*

The participant's voice and body language were recorded, and the virtual child was programmed to gradually stop crying and show curiosity about what the adult was saying to them.

Next, the adult re-experienced the scene, but now from the child's perspective. The adult looked at the recorded real life avatar of herself, who approached her and said the same compassionate things with kind gestures – a technique called 'embodiment'. After a number of repetitions of this mini-intervention of eight minutes in a month-long period, the participants reported that they had become kinder toward themselves, and that their symptoms of depression had reduced. Some told researchers that they thought about the experience when they were upset, and it helped them to be more compassionate with themselves.[7,8]

Just as we provide comfort to children when they are in pain, so we can provide comfort when we ourselves are in pain. According to Kristin Neff[9], self-compassion consists of three parts:

1. Recognising and mindfully opening ourselves to the emotional pain.
2. Reminding ourselves that suffering connects us, against our tendency to be ashamed and to isolate ourselves when something goes wrong.

3. Responding with self-kindness instead of self-criticism, realising that we need compassion and deserve it.

If you find that you're stressed or in emotional pain, you can try saying the following sentences to yourself:

> 'This is a moment of suffering' (or 'This is really hard')
> 'Suffering is a part of life' (or 'I'm not the only one suffering')
> 'I will be kind to myself'
> 'I will give myself the compassion I need'

It's important to note that we practice self-compassion not because we expect it to make us magically feel better, but because it helps us cope with feeling bad[4]. Trying to use self-compassion as a way to resist or to get rid of difficult feelings is doomed to failure. We need to understand that suffering is a normal part of being human, and is allowed. To quote compassion teacher Chris Germer:

> 'Compassion gives us the strength to abide with the vicissitudes of our lives – pleasure and pain, sickness and health, gain and loss – until we have an opportunity to change them.'[4]

Self-compassion is learning to be our own parent, and learning to take care of the child within us. For parents who didn't receive sufficient care and comfort when they themselves were young, self-compassion can be challenging. A young mother from the virtual reality self-compassion experiment discussed above[6] described her experience of an exercise in which she had to visualize being held and comforted by someone who made her feel safe:

> 'I've never had anyone who would hold me like that. Sad, but it felt so good.'

In one of my courses, we ran a self-compassion exercise in which parents had to hold in mind someone who loved them unconditionally. One participant had lost her mother as a young child. For the exercise, she chose her adoptive mother, and cried at the image of this person holding, caressing and listening to her. She said:

> 'I know what it is, that sadness, that fear. Someone loving you unconditionally – deep inside, I find that scary. I lost the first person who did it with me.'

Compassion, the feeling that arises when we witness suffering in others and sparks the desire to help, is not the same as empathy, which is feeling someone else's emotion.[10] To truly experience compassion, we must realize that we are separate from the person who suffers, and that their suffering is not our own.

This distinction between empathy and compassion can help us understand the phenomenon of so-called *compassion fatigue*. Parents who care for a child with a severe condition, or deal with other family circumstances related to the suffering of others like a partner with an addiction or a parent with dementia, can suffer from compassion fatigue. Charles Figley defines compassion fatigue as follows:

> *'A state that is experienced by those who help humans or animals in need; an extreme tension and preoccupation with the suffering of those who are helped, such that this can cause traumatic stress in the helper.'[11]*

Compassion fatigue is frequently seen in helpers or parents of those in traumatic situations, and is sometimes called 'secondary traumatisation'. Mother Teresa recognized this risk among her nuns, who were caring for people in great need, so every five years she sent them away on a one-year restorative sabbatical. Because parents identify so closely with their children, the risk of compassion fatigue when caring for a child with severe problems is high[12], and it is essential that we take good care of ourselves whenever we are confronted with family trauma and suffering.

Compassion fatigue is not only caused by witnessing suffering and trauma in itself, but also by how we respond to it. As parents, in order to be able to truly connect to the suffering of our child, it is important not only to remember that our child's suffering is not our own, but also that we do have our own suffering to cope with. Our suffering is the suffering of a parent witnessing the discomfort of their child, and we need to give ourselves self-compassion for it[4].

In the groups I facilitate, I have observed how parents who suffer due to the suffering of their children (which may relate to the consequences of autism, addiction, anorexia, suicidality, divorce or any number of other factors), often blame themselves for having made mistakes which contributed to the present situation. Apportioning this self-blame may be a psychological mechanism that helps them deal with a sense of guilt, by serving penance.

Irrespective of whether or not it could have been prevented (about which more in Chapter 8), it is parents who suffer most from the suffering of our children. We need compassion, and we can give it to ourselves. So why don't we do it, when we need it most? We'd rather take on our child's pain so they don't suffer anymore. This is understandable, but true compassion means understanding that the pain is theirs, not ours. We can recognize that our children suffer and we can feel for them, but we can't always alleviate their pain or feel how much it hurts. True compassion means allowing the child's pain to exist, while at the same time taking care of our own suffering.

We can also take care of ourselves by seeing the child within us, and recognising what he or she needs. As children, we all depended on our parents. Sometimes when we were sad, afraid, angry, upset or jealous, we may have found that our parents, or others who cared for us, offered not comfort but reproval (*'It was your own fault'*; *'If only you hadn't…'*; *'You shouldn't feel like that'*). Perhaps they were right; or perhaps they reacted like that because they themselves struggled with self-compassion. We don't make mistakes on purpose, yet we're often judged as if we did. I remember that as a child I once lost a 100-Guilder banknote, which I'd put in my trouser pocket. Cycling home, I was terrified of my parents' response, and blamed myself for being stupid. Tellingly, I no longer remember their actual reaction – only my own fear and self-blame.

If similar things happen to me today, as an adult – like the time when I left my suitcase on a bus at Schiphol airport because I was talking on the phone, and in my unsuccessful efforts to recover it missed a flight to Oxford – my first impulse is still to blame myself for being stupid. However, this only worsens the suffering; what I really need is self-compassion (*'This is a moment of suffering'*; *'I'm not the only one who has ever lost their suitcase'*; *'I'll be kind to myself'*). So I resist the impulse to blame myself, and I give myself the self-compassion that I deserve.

Meditation teacher Thich Nhat Hanh uses the image of a baby to help us be kind to ourselves. If you're very angry, for example, you must treat yourself with extreme kindness and rock yourself like a baby. According to Thich Nhat Hanh, inside each one of us is a wounded child who can be healed by self-compassion[13]:

> *'When we speak of listening with compassion, we usually think of listening to someone else. But we must also listen to the wounded child inside of us. Sometimes the wounded child in us needs all our attention. That little child might emerge from the depths of your consciousness and ask for your attention. If you are mindful, you will hear his or her voice calling for help. At that moment, instead of paying attention to whatever is in front of you, go back and tenderly embrace the wounded child. You can talk directly to the child with*

the language of love, saying, "In the past, I left you alone. I went away from you. Now, I am very sorry. I am going to embrace you". You can say, "Darling, I am here for you. I will take good care of you. I know that you suffer so much. I have been so busy. I have neglected you, and now I have learned a way to come back to you". If necessary, you have to cry together with that child. Whenever you need to, you can sit and breathe with the child. "Breathing in, I go back to my wounded child; breathing out, I take good care of my wounded child".'

By regularly practicing the bodyscan meditation (Exercise 2.1), we can learn to listen to our bodies and take better care of them. We can also ask *'What do I need?'* (Exercise 2.2). By practising other meditations such as the hand on heart (Exercise 2.3), or by simply saying compassionate things to ourselves, we can cultivate self-compassion. It is important to realize that it is the practice itself that matters: allowing space to wish ourselves health, happiness and love. It doesn't matter whether we ever receive the things we wish ourselves. By focusing each day on things we're grateful for (Exercise 2.4), no matter how small, we can remind ourselves that happiness isn't in the future; it's here and now.

Exercises

Exercise 2.1: Bodyscan with self-compassion (audio track 2)

The bodyscan is a meditation that you can do sitting or lying down.

Generally speaking we live inside our heads, and have little awareness of our bodies until something goes wrong. In this meditation, you'll scan the different parts of your body with your attention. Do this with a *beginner's mind*, with open curious attention for all sensations, as if this is the first time you've ever noticed your body.

Taking time to pay attention to our whole body is not only a practice in attention and awareness; it's also an act of self-compassion. This week, try to do a bodyscan every day. Audio track 2 contains a 10-minute bodyscan. If you prefer a longer one, there are plenty to be found online by mindfulness teachers such as Jon Kabat-Zinn or Mark Williams. Make notes about your experience if you wish.

A warning about feeling guilty when you don't meditate:

You might *intend* to meditate every day, just as you might plan to exercise, eat healthy foods, drink less alcohol or have an early night. Regardless, a day is likely to come when you don't meditate. This can be a source of feelings of guilt or failure, and self-blame, which will take you further from meditating. If feelings of guilt and failure are left unchecked, meditation will soon become just another thing on the 'to do' list, making your already busy life even busier and leading ultimately to this book being thrown into a bin!

Therefore, when you find yourself skipping the daily meditation, consider making a list of all the potential obstacles to practice, and solutions for each one. Here's an example of a list that I and a group of other mindfulness trainers made about our own obstacles and solutions:

Obstacle	Solution
Too tired	Get more sleep; meditate at other times of day
Too busy, no time	Cancel non-essential tasks; ask others to help
Not looking forward to it	It doesn't have to be fun to be beneficial
Forgot	Set reminder on phone; plan into day
Find it boring	Trust that with practice it will get more interesting
Too repetitive	Try different audio meditations
Fear of doing it wrong	There isn't a 'right way', and it's okay to be nervous
Have drunk alcohol	Do it anyway; meditate at other times of day
Feel guilty	My family, colleagues and friends will benefit!
It isn't helping	Give it more time

Exercise 2.2: What do I need?

Stopping to ask 'What do I need?' is, according to Chris Germer,[14] the first step toward self-compassion in your daily life. Ask yourself the following questions and write the answers in your notebook. Below each question is a sample answer.

Question: How do I already take care of myself as a parent? (physically, mentally, emotionally, relationally and spiritually)

Sample answer: Once a week I take my children to my mother to have an afternoon for myself. I meditate early each morning before waking the children, I ask my partner to help me, and I read books about parenting.

Question*: What new ways can I think of to take care of myself as a parent? (physically, mentally, emotionally, relationally and spiritually)*

Sample answer: I can teach my children to take my feelings into account. I can be more in tune with my own feelings and bodily sensations while I'm doing things with my children. If I ever find I'm stuck, I can call a friend.

Exercise 2.3: Hand on heart and loving kindness meditation

This week, try to notice moments of parental suffering. It can be small things, for example that you did your best to make a nice meal and your children wouldn't eat it, or that by forgetting a birthday party you made your child angry and sad.

- Say to yourself: *'This is a moment of suffering'*.

- Connect your suffering with that of other parents, by saying to yourself: *'I'm not the only one who suffers'*, or *'I'm not the only parent who makes mistakes'*.

- Say comforting words to yourself, like: *'It's not easy to be a good parent'*, or: *'I'll be kind to myself'*. See what consoling phrases you can think of, and write them down.

Or try comforting actions, such as:

- Put both hands on the area where you heart is, and feel the pressure and warmth from one hand on the other and from both hands on your chest. Continue to experience this feeling for as long as you want.

- Embrace yourself by wrapping both arms around yourself.

- Embryo position: Lay down on your side, curled up, with your arms around your legs in a protective posture.

- Rub your hands together until they are warm; then put them on your face.

Alternatively, ask yourself the question: *'What do I need now?'* and see what comes up. Irrespective of whether you can receive what you need or give it to yourself at that moment, it helps to connect to your broader ongoing needs for care, support, kindness, silence, rest and comfort.

27

Exercise 2.4: Gratitude

This week, before you go to sleep each night, write in your notebook three things that happened during the day that you were grateful for, no matter how small. Keep the notebook on your bedside cabinet as a reminder! I've done this ever since I participated in a workshop given by Chris Germer,[14] and even on difficult days I notice that it makes me aware of what Jon Kabat-Zinn calls the *'little things that ain't so little'*. It helps me to celebrate life, and to end each day well.

Thich Nhat Hanh[15] says: *'We all have the seeds of love and compassion in us, but also the seeds of hatred and anger. The more we water the seeds of love and compassion, the more love and compassion we create for ourselves and others.'*

Mindfulness can help us to water the right seeds.

References

1   Naht Hahn, T. (2003). *Creating true peace: Ending violence in yourself, your family, your community and the world*. New York: Atria Books.

2   Maex, E. (2008). *Mindfulness: In de maalstroom van je leven*. Houten: Lannoo.

3   Siegel, D., & Hartzell, M. (2003). *Parenting from the inside out*. New York: Tarcher.

4   Neff, K.D. (2012). The science of self-compassion. In Germer, C. K., & Siegel, R. D. (Eds.). *Wisdom and Compassion in Psychotherapy: Deepening mindfulness in clinical practice*. New York: Guilford Press.

5   Brouwers, J. (1983). *De laatste deur: Essays over zelfmoord in de Nederlandstalige letteren*. Amsterdam: Synopsis.

6   Itkowitz C., (2016). The surprising way researchers are using virtual reality to beat depression. *The Washington Post*. Available at: https://www.washingtonpost.com/news/inspired-life/wp/2016/02/17/how-comforting-a-crying-child-in-virtual-reality-can-treat-depression-in-real-life/ (accessed January 2020).

7   Falconer, C. J., Rovira, A., King, J. A., Gilbert, P., Antley, A., Fearon, P., Ralph, N., Slater, M., & Brewin, C. R. (2016). Embodying self-compassion within virtual reality and its effects on patients with depression. *British Journal of Psychiatry Open*, **2**,74-80.

8   Falconer, C. J., Slater, M., Rovira, A., King, J. A., Gilbert, P., Antley, A., & Brewin, C. R. (2014). Embodying compassion: a virtual reality paradigm for overcoming excessive self-criticism. *PloS one*, **9**, 1-7.

9   Neff, K. (2011). *Self-Compassion*. New York: William Morrow.

10 Goetz, J. L., Keltner, D., & Simon-Thomas, E. (2010). Compassion: an evolutionary analysis and empirical review. *Psychological Bulletin*, **136**, 351

11 Figley, C.R., (1995). Compassion fatigue: Toward a new understanding of the costs of caring. In Stamm, B.H. (Ed.) *Secondary traumatic stress: Self-care issues for clinicians, researchers, and educators*. (pp. 3-28). Baltimore, USA: The Sidran Press.

12 Salmela-Aro, K., Tynkkynen, L., & Vuori, J. (2011). Parents' work burn-out and adolescents' school burn-out: Are they shared? *European Journal of Developmental Psychology*, **8**, 215-227.

13 Nhat Hanh, T. (2010) *Healing the inner child*. Berkeley: Parallel Press.

14 Germer, C. (2012). Personal communication, November.

15 Nhat Hanh, T. (2009). *Happiness*. Berkeley: Parallel Press.

Chapter 3:
Parental stress: From surviving to breathing space

'She [Vanja, 4 years old] *is already practiced in the ways of the world and can be so cheeky that I completely lose my head and sometimes shout at her or shake her until she starts crying. But usually she just laughs. The last time it happened, the last time I was so furious I shook her and she just laughed, I had a sudden inspiration and placed my hand on her chest. Her heart was pounding. Oh, my, how it was pounding.'*
Karl Ove Knausgård[1]

Because I live in a city close to a busy crèche, I'm occasionally treated to the stress of parents dropping off their children. Perhaps they're late for work, or can't find a parking spot, or the kids woke early and won't cooperate. In the evening, when the children are collected, the stress seems to be even worse: maybe it's the race against time, as the crèche closes at 6.30pm sharp (and what will happen if you aren't there?!). The children are tired and misbehaving, so the parents issue threats (*'If you don't stop crying, we won't go to the park'*) or try to compromise (*'If you stop crying, we'll go out to eat!'*).

Now, imagine if the crèche door opened not with a passcode, but when a parent sat in silence for a minute or a sensor registered a calm heartbeat. What a difference! Parents would be forced to assess their own mental state, and would drop off or collect off their children with a much more open, considered mind.

The stress of childcare can bring out the worst in us. When we lose our patience and let frustration and anger take over we usually come to regret it deeply, as we know that these moments can affect a young person in negative ways that we remember from our own childhood. Karl Ove Knausgård[1] wrote a series of six loosely autobiographical books in which he described a father who, in stress, often lost patience and the effect it had on his children.

This chapter is about parental stress – its evolutionary basis and function, and the lack of control we have over it ('*We can't help it, we were made this way!*'). However, we'll also discuss how recognizing this stress and focusing on experiencing it can prevent us shooting into 'survival mode' when there is no real danger present. By learning this skill, we can become aware of our parenting responses instead of simply acting on instinct. In short, we can choose how we react.

Few things can cause us more stress than when something is wrong with our child. I remember going to work shortly after my maternity leave, leaving our three-month old son with a babysitter, and being told as soon as I arrived that there was an urgent problem and I should phone home immediately. I began to assume the worst: '*My child is dead*'; '*He's had an accident*'; '*He's sick*'. It turned out I'd forgotten to leave the babysitter a note about what groceries needed to be bought for dinner.

This example shows how our so-called *danger schema*[2] can be activated instantly by unclear messages like '*There's something urgent*'. A schema is an organized cluster of knowledge and experience related to a theme. The danger schema relates to risk and danger, and is usually present early in life. It is activated by particular signals – these might be physical feelings (stress), words (urgent), pictures (ambulance), or even memories ('*my brother's accident when he was ten*').

We've evolved to give high priority to danger signals (urgent) and catastrophic interpretations ('*my child is dead*') above harmless or positive ones, because the potential costs of ignoring danger that turns out to be real are far higher than the potential costs of worrying when no actual danger exists.

Whenever we detect something potentially dangerous like a rustling in the grass that might be a snake, this signal takes an 'express route' through our brain – skipping the prefrontal cortex where we calculate, consider possibilities and see the perspectives of others. The express route fast tracks the signal to the amygdala and our limbic system – primitive areas that are also active when we face born (e.g. falling) and learned (e.g. spiders) fears. This allows us to take action instantly without having to think it through, so we can immediately jump away from the danger.

This ability to act instantly in dangerous situations helped our ancestors survive. It is a *fight or flight* response, whereby we instinctively decide what will give us the best chance of survival: to fight or to run away[3]. We don't have control over this – it happens automatically and ultimately prioritizes the survival of our genes. Because our children carry our genes, they activate our danger schema far more often than other stimuli and are one of our greatest sources of stress. It is worth noting that this can vary by gender, as only a mother can be sure a child is hers and men can have many more children than women.

A great deal of research has been conducted into the fight or flight response, especially with men, but recent research has shown that another response is common in women: *tend and befriend*[4,5]. In stressful situations women, far more than men, often try to connect with others. They'll keep their children with them (tend) or smile at an attacker (befriend) if it increases their chance of survival. This may help to explain why mothers, after a stressful divorce, sometimes keep children away from their father, and why women who are raped can afterwards wonder why they were so nice to their assailant.

Let's now look at everyday parent-child interactions and situations where parents can become stressed. It might be that one of your children, despite several warnings, is on their phone in the morning instead of concentrating on getting ready, causing her siblings to be late for school and you for work. Or perhaps your teenager has come home with a poor grade because he didn't study hard enough for a test. Or it could be any other everyday interaction with your children that regularly causes you stress!

Where do you feel that stress in your body? Maybe your heart beats faster, or your breathing becomes shallow? Maybe you feel suddenly warm or cold? Maybe your muscles tense, or your throat gets dry? What emotions do you notice? Anxiety? Fear? Irritation? Anger? Disappointment? Sadness? What thoughts pop up? Do you think your child is lazy or selfish, or that they're causing trouble just to spite you? Maybe you think they'll fail their exams, and ultimately it will be your fault, but you can't constantly push and organize everything for everyone all the time. Or maybe you're just a bad parent…

What do you think would be your first impulse in a situation like that? Not how you think you'd really respond, but your first *impulse* to act? In the late for school scenario, you might feel an urge to grab your child and drag them to the door, or pull the phone forcibly from their hand. Maybe you'd want to shout at them, to make them feel bad for their siblings who were ready on time. Or maybe you'd just want to give up and leave without them, or go back to bed and hide under the covers. In the case of the failed test, you might want to preach to your child about their future, pointing out that they'll have to fend for themselves one day, or threaten them with extra tutoring. Maybe you'd want to give up and let them work it out on their own. Or maybe you'd just want to keep out of it, or call your child lazy, or compare them to others who work hard to get good grades.

Now let's look at these stressful situations and responses from an evolutionary perspective. Imagine that your child runs into the street and a car is coming. That will provoke the physical stress response: increased heart rate, fast shallow breathing, sweating, muscles tensing and so on. These signs indicate that the stress hormone adrenaline is active, and the body is ready for fight or flight. How would you react? Scream at your child? Pull them off the street? Any such instant response, triggered without any conscious thought, will have the intended effect: your child will survive.

Of course, the difference between this example and situations of morning school runs or test results is that the latter aren't matters of life or death. In these scenarios the triggers are everyday parental problems, yet the body reacts in just the same way and with the same physical reactions as when facing real danger. So the signals take the same express route through our brain, skipping the prefrontal cortex and allowing us to act on an instant fight or flight decision.

The problem with this is that, in non-threatening situations, acting on instinct doesn't always help us achieve our goal. In fact, instant reactions can be bad for the parent-child relationship. For example, screaming at a child might cause more conflict and confusion. No matter how good our intentions, if we lose patience and insult our child, strike them, slam doors, walk away from them or just behave in intimidating or unpredictable ways, it can have a lasting effect and cause long-term damage to the relationship. (In Chapter 5 we'll discuss how to deal with possible damage after a falling out with your child.)

One thing that distinguishes humans from other mammals is that, when faced with stressful situations, we can do more than just react: we can think. Unfortunately this isn't always helpful, as we tend to worry, ruminate, imagine the worst and take things personally – all of which can cause more harm in already stressful situations. Although research by Tom Borkovec[6,7] surprisingly reveals that mulling over negative thoughts can sometimes reduce stress, as we also create an opportunity to think of solutions and explanations, generally speaking worrying is bad for us.

Moreover, we pay a high price for our tendency to worry. By dwelling on problems we prevent ourselves from letting go, and become trapped in feelings of guilt, melancholy, powerlessness and despair. This is a key reason why humans suffer from so many stress-related illnesses. Meditation teacher Eckhart Tolle[8] has explored the power of thinking. He explains how we can become absorbed in our own thoughts, and shows that if we rehearse the same thoughts over and again we will eventually come to believe them. In fact, he estimates that 90% of all our thinking is completely unnecessary!

The negative thoughts that can occur during times of parental stress are well shown by this zen-koan[7] (a koan is a question or riddle used to provoke doubt and test progress):

Question 1:
What is the sound of one hand clapping?
Answer:
The sound of one hand clapping is the sound of one hand clapping.

Question 2:
What is the sound of a child misbehaving?
Answer:
The sound of a child misbehaving is the sound of a child misbehaving.

Question 3:
What is the sound of my child misbehaving?
Answer:
The sound of my child misbehaving is the sound of '*I cannot control my child*'; the sound of '*I should be able to*'; the sound of '*I am a bad parent*'; the sound of '*I don't know what to do*'; the sound of '*I hate this child*'; the sound of '*I should not feel this way*'; and the sound of my failure.[9]

To summarize, humans have evolved to detect danger quickly, and to think the worst when faced with vague signals or stressful situations. When our children are involved, this response is heightened and extends to non-threatening situations. In such scenarios we may react instantly with a fight or flight response that serves no real purpose. We may also begin to dwell on the situation in an attempt to control our stress, which only makes things worse. This all happens automatically and we can't control it. Yet it can harm our children! So what can we do about it?

The answer lies in becoming aware of our stress. By paying careful attention to our bodies, we can learn to recognize stress when it happens. With meditation, we can become more attuned to what is going on in our body and our instinctive responses. For example, with sitting meditation we can learn to feel an itch, to notice our instinctive response to scratch it, and to understand that doing so will probably just make it worse.

By becoming aware of ourselves during stress and observing what happens in our bodies, we can avoid the express route signal preparing our fight or flight response. Practising this awareness, and perceiving stress on a metacognitive level (thinking about how we think), allows us to give ourselves a moment of time and space – and this can be enough to prevent the express route signal and activate the conscious part of our brain.

Noticing the instinctive responses that accompany heightened tension allows us to delay our automatic reactions and look at situations with a so-called beginner's mind. This enables us to consider not only our own point of view but also that of others, and to visualize the consequences of our actions before we take them. In this manner, we can create the space needed to react in alternative ways, and to choose a rational answer instead of acting on instinct. Of course, you can still choose to drag your child to school if you wish! However, these days I always notice in myself the difference between considered and reactive anger, with the latter usually reflecting my own state of mind.

Regular meditation can also help to lower our general stress levels. We can all make it part of our daily routine, just like brushing our teeth. Meditation is maintenance of the soul, and for this reason it's important to allow time and space for it every day – to have a period not of doing, but of simply being. This may initially cause some internal struggles: you may think you don't have time for it, feel too tired, find it boring, think it won't help, or feel guilty about sitting doing nothing. However, in order to enjoy the benefits of meditation it's important just to do it. So, just as we always brush our teeth without questioning whether we feel like it or whether we have time, so meditation too can be planned for a set time and become part of our everyday self-care routine.

Exercises

Exercise 3.1: Sitting meditation with attention for sounds and thoughts (audio track 3)

In this meditation we open ourselves to sounds, sounds in the room, sounds in our body, and sounds from outside. Listening to sounds with a beginner's mind, without labelling 'bird', 'car', 'child', but listening to rhythm, tone, volume, timbre, location of the sound, whether it moves or stays. Then we let go of attention for sounds to observe our thoughts (images, memories, inner dialogue, planning) from a distance. Seeing thoughts as thoughts rather than the truth, not identifying with the thoughts. We discover the power of our thinking, how our thinking can immediately bring us in another mood state, and how much of our thinking had no purpose, and takes us out of our direct experience.

Exercise 3.2: Breathing space (audio track 4)

Check twice a day how you are, at moments you remember, or by setting a timer on your mobile phone. The practice takes about three minutes, one minute per step. You can use track 4 the first few times.

1. **Checking in**

Take a position that helps you enlarge the attention for this moment; it can be sitting, standing, lying. Close your eyes if you want. Focus your attention on your inner experience. Notice which physical sensations, emotions, thoughts are present, and whether you feel an urge to do something. Give words to your experience. For example: *'there is anger'*, *'self-critical thoughts are present'*, *'thirst'*, *'tendency to get up'*. Say to yourself: whatever it is, it is ok, let me feel it.

2. **Attention to breathing**

Now bring your full attention to your breathing. Follow each breath the whole way in and the whole way out. No need to change your breathing in any way, just following the soft rhythm… breath after breath.

3. **Widening the attention**

Widen your attention now to your whole body, including any discomfort. A sense as if your whole body is breathing. Feeling the length, width, volume, weight of the body, sitting, standing or lying here. Be aware of your posture, your facial expression. Take this more focused awareness as best as you can to the next moments of your day.

Exercise 3.3: Observing parental stress

This week, pay attention to experiences of parental stress. Notice moments of stress in situations related to your child, and observe what happens in your body and what impulses you have. Do this with an open, curious, non-judgmental attitude, and notice any negative or self-destructive thoughts you have about your physical stress levels and their accompanying impulses.

Focus too on identifying signs that you are about to enter parental stress mode – then you will be able to head this off by taking a breathing space, asking yourself what you need in this situation (see Exercise 2.2), or performing a hand-on-heart meditation (see Exercise 2.3). You can also ask your partner or children to help you recognize these signs, and if they spot them to give you an agreed signal to withdraw in order to feel what is happening to you, and if needed take a breathing space.

Here are seven questions to fill out in your notebook whenever you enter parental stress mode, along with sample answers.

1. What is the situation?
   'My child has a school test tomorrow but has forgotten what he needs to do, and now he's afraid to call a friend and ask for help.'

2. What is going on in my body?
   'Hot, palpitations, sweating.'

3. What emotions do I notice?
   'Anxiety, annoyance, anger.'

4. What thoughts occur?
   'He won't do well at school or in life if he carries on like this; he does this sort of thing on purpose to create problems for me; I don't deserve this.'

5. What action impulses do I notice?
   'Impulse to take over angrily; impulse to walk away; impulse to shout.'

6. Breathing space or self-compassion applied?
   'Yes, I took a breathing space.'

7. Effect?
   'Although I'm annoyed, I do feel sorry for him too; he tries hard, and I'm aware that I'm worried.'

References

1   Knausgard, K. O. (2012). *My struggle. Book one*. New York: Archipelago Books.

2   Mathews, A., & Macleod, C. (1985). Selective processing of threat cues in anxiety states. *Behaviour research and therapy*, **23**, 563-569.

3   LeDoux, J. (1996). The emotional brain: The mysterious underpinnings of emotional life. New York: Simon and Schuster.

4   Taylor, S.E., Cousino Klein, L., Lewis, B.P., Gruenewald, T.L., Gurung, R.A.R., & Updegraff, J.A. (2000). Biobehavioral responses to stress in females: Tend-and-befriend, not fight-or-flight. *Psychological Review*, **107**, 411-429.

5   Turton, S., & Campbell, C. (2005). Tend and befriend versus fight or flight: Gender differences in behavioral response to stress among university students. *Journal of Applied Biobehavioral Research*, **10**, 209-232.

6   Borkovec, T. D., Alcaine, O., & Behar, E. (2004). Avoidance theory of worry and generalized anxiety disorder. *Generalized anxiety disorder: Advances in research and practice*. New York: Guilford Press.

7   McLaughlin, K. A., Borkovec, T. D., & Sibrava, N. J. (2007). The effects of worry and rumination on affect states and cognitive activity. *Behavior Therapy*, **38**, 23-38.

8   Tolle, E. (1999). *The power of now: A guide to spiritual enlightenment*. San Francisco, USA: New World Library.

9   Coyne. L.W. & Wilson, K.G. (2004). The role of cognitive fusion in impaired parenting: An RFT analysis. *International Journal of Psychology and Psychological Therapy*, **4**, 468-486.

Chapter 4: Parental expectations and the true nature of the child

Infinite Possibilities

'You do not know the true origin of your children.

*You call them yours
but they belong to a greater Mystery.*

*You do not know the name of this Mystery,
but it is the true Mother and Father of your children.*

At birth your children are filled with possibilities.

It is not your job to limit these possibilities.

*Do not say, 'This and that are possible
for you.*

These other things are not.'

They will discover on their own what is and is not possible.

*It is your job to help them stay open
to the marvellous mysteries of life.*

It may be interesting to ask,

*'What limitations have I, unthinking,
taken upon myself?'*

*It is very difficult for your child's horizons
to be greater than your own.*

*Do something today that pushes
against your own preconceptions.*

*Then take your child's hand
and gently encourage her to do the same.'*

The Parent's Tao Te Ching[1]

In my family, it was important to be a high achiever. My sister recently reminded me that if our average school grade was a seven we'd be 'whole milk', while an eight would make you the 'cream'. She remembered that she was whole milk and I was cream, and I could still feel her pain over the comparison. Yet I don't remember being praised as the 'cream'; I only remember that she was better than me at many other things, like sport.

My parents and siblings all excelled at sports. They made teams, won prizes and had great stamina, particularly at hockey and ice-skating. I mainly remember how cold and wet I was playing hockey; how I was scared of being hit by the ball, worried that my passes would go astray and uncomfortable showering with the other girls. I remember how embarrassing it was to lose to my younger siblings at a skating competition, and their laughter when I fell over yet again. I much preferred sitting in my warm, comfortable room, writing in my diary or listening to music. Only now, almost half a century later, do I realize that this was just as important for my development. Yet I don't remember my parents ever seeming interested in what I got up to alone in my room.

For most parents, when their first child arrives he or she seems perfect. However, this initial idealization can lead to feelings of disappointment later, as the child develops and grows up. Brené Brown, a researcher and writer of many books about vulnerability, perfectionism and embarrassment[2], once said in a popular TED talk: *'We should hold our newborn child and say: "You are an imperfect human (as we all are), but you deserve my unconditional love and attention".'*[3]

If a child shows talent for piano playing, we fantasize about his first performance. If she writes well, we see a future author. If he is good at thinking things through we think of an academic career, and if she plays a lot of football we imagine her as a professional player. We all secretly hope that our children will have special talents and that we'll also receive indirect praise for them *'He got that from me!'*.

The grades our child achieves, the university they may attend, the job they get, how pretty, popular, smart, sporty, creative or otherwise talented they prove to be – as parents we assume that, with our child's success, our own social standing will also increase. If our child isn't successful, we expect it to reflect negatively on us. When other parents tell us how well their children are doing, it can be difficult just to be happy for their success and enjoy their parental pride. Subconsciously we tend to compare their situation with our own and feel smaller as a result.

The Buddhist concept of *Anatta* ('no self') can help us with this. According to Anatta, there is no unchanging, permanent part of the self. Ron Siegel explains it like this:

'If we keep exercising the simple practice of mindfulness, we will find that our impression of a coherent, permanent self is just an illusion, kept alive by our constant internal monologue revolving around this 'me'. From everyday decisions such as choosing what to have for dinner up to existential fears of deadly illnesses, this constant monologue fills our every waking hour. By constantly listening to this, we start believing that this drama must have a protagonist. However, if we keep practicing mindfulness long and frequently enough, this image of personal worth can be unravelled. In reality, we never truly encounter that small, heroic man or woman, that stable impression of 'me' that we see so often in our thoughts.'[4]

How would we experience parenthood if we were to examine it from the idea of Anatta? To realize that there is no real, unchanging 'I, me and mine'? That these aren't *my* children, but simply children? That this isn't *my* family, just a family? And that it isn't *my* parenting, just parenting? How would this affect our expectations for our children? Think of their education for example – how much of our expectations for their schooling is based on our own education and our parents' expectations, and the expectations of their parents before them?

When we realize that there is no true self and our children aren't 'ours', even if they share genetic material with us, we can stop seeing ourselves as all-important, and stop constantly comparing ourselves and our children with others. This lets us finally start paying attention to what our children actually experience, and what truly moves and inspires them – not just their wish to meet our expectations. To practice mindful parenting is to get to know the true nature of our child, instead of seeing them as an extension of ourselves and projecting our own expectations on to them. Many of these expectations are often the same ones given to us by our own parents, and that we ourselves could not live up to.

But how do parental expectations affect a child? All children want love and attention, and when they realize that these tend to follow whenever they live up to our expectations, they will try their best to achieve the goals we set. Writer Griet Op de Beeck once said: *'There is no unconditional love from parents to their children, only unconditional love from children to their parents. Because our children are completely dependent on us and love us unconditionally, they will try to focus on things that please us. However, by doing so they risk losing their own authenticity – they risk losing themselves'.*[5] Or to quote professor of Literature Joseph Campbell: *'If we follow someone else's way, we will not reach our potential'.*[6]

My daughter's Latin teacher once told me that he'd helped her deal with performance anxiety, which she doesn't believe she has. I was curious as to how he'd supposedly done this. He explained: *'Zero per cent transference!'* Now, as a psychotherapist I know the term transference – patients can project feelings, wishes and experiences, especially related to their parents, onto their therapist when they try to push away their own traits or emotions. The idea that teachers can also project onto their students wasn't something I had considered before. I probably looked confused, so he continued: *'I've learned to stop expecting a lot from her, just because she is so smart'*. This made me stop and think – and taught me an important lesson about the expectations that I myself project onto my daughter.

Let's become more aware of the expectations we place on our children and ourselves, those placed on us by our parents, and even those that were placed on our parents by their parents. Let's consider how they've influenced us, negatively and positively. Every child wants their parents to be happy with them just the way they are, to be praised, and not to have to earn their parents' love. They want to be accepted for themselves. This is the same unconditional love we search for in romantic partners, and that our partners hope to find in us.

Practicing mindfulness can help us step back and observe our thoughts instead of identifying with them. This in turn can help us become aware of how much we worry about our social standing in the groups we identify with. Who lives in the biggest house, dresses best, has the most attractive partner, leads the most interesting life and has the funniest friends? And as a parent: whose children behave best in public, whose are the smartest, prettiest, richest, sportiest and most popular? The problem is, although we can feel a burst of happiness at being better than others at some things, there will always be other things we're worse at and other people who are even better than us. The goal is not to be perfect but to be whole, which means developing different parts of ourselves.

When our child comes home disappointed because he wasn't selected for the football team, we might try to cheer him up by saying: *'Never mind, you're top of the class and a great runner!'* But as parents, it might actually be more helpful if we could share our experience of failure, perhaps by giving an example from our own childhood: *'I remember how it felt to be chosen last during games at school. I felt small and like nobody wanted to be around me. It really hurt'*. This way, we can truly connect with the suffering of our child. If I can recall what I was going through and what I needed when I was waiting to be chosen and ended up last again, than I may understand what my child is going through and how I can help.

Moreover, if we never address the pain we felt as a child, we'll tend to avoid it when reacting in adulthood. This won't help when our child encounters a similar situation. I used to tell myself '*I might not be good at volleyball, but I'm cleverer than them!*' to mask the pain of not being chosen. But now, if I tell my child the same, I'm not only continuing to avoid my own pain but teaching them not to take care of their pain either. The part of the brain that is activated when we feel left out is the same one that is activated by physical pain. Being excluded really hurts! An experiment has even shown that taking an aspirin after being socially excluded lessens the pain.[7] The aspirin against rejection is comfort and support, which you can ask from another but also give to yourself via self-compassion.

When we think of expectations we mostly imagine unrealistic, lofty goals that can cause anxiety and stress. However, low expectations can also hinder a child's development. When parents don't support a child's interests and ambitions – for example by dissuading them from going to university because they aren't from a graduate background – that too is failing to recognize the true nature of their child.

Stereotypical expectations can also harm children. Girls growing up with only sisters have been shown to develop farther than girls from mixed families, since fathers instinctively focus their expectations on boys. The same is true for all-female schools – girls accomplish more because at mixed schools teachers expect most from the boys. Experimental research shows that both fathers and mothers, when their three year olds perform tasks in a lab (e.g. throwing a ball, completing a puzzle), give their sons more positive feedback and their daughters more negative, even if both did just as well.[8] Negative parental feedback also correlated to more shame in toddlers when doing these tasks. This kind of research shows how our expectations as parents are skewed by factors such as background and gender stereotypes, and how this can impact our children.

To summarize, parents tend to 'project' expectations onto their children that don't fit the true nature of the child and which can hinder their development. These expectations often spring from a self-oriented focus, in which we see our children as extensions of ourselves. They may also be based on expectations for ourselves that we were not able to live up to, and thus hope to achieve through our children, and on the expectations that our parents had for us. They are strongly affected by cultural factors such as gender stereotypes.

Children are independent beings with a right to their own development, and we shouldn't burden them with the weight of our expectations. As Albert Einstein said:

'If people are good only because they fear punishment, and hope for reward, then we are a sorry lot indeed.'

Exercises:

Exercise 4.1: Seeing meditation

Sit or stand in front of a window for a five-minute seeing meditation (set an alarm).

First, close your eyes for a moment and take time to feel how your body is sitting or standing, and where it makes contact with the ground. Then, open your eyes and look outside with a beginner's mind, as if you're seeing this view for the first time. Try to look as closely as you can without labelling things – so don't think 'bird', 'tree' or 'car', but instead just look at forms, light, shadow, colour, movement. You can zoom in on details then zoom back out again to see the whole view.

Notice if your attention lingers on things, perhaps because you find them beautiful while ignoring things you don't find attractive. Try to let go of all your pre-formed judgements of whether particular things are beautiful or not, and practice *equanimity* by taking in everything you see and welcoming it all.

Also be aware of how you feel during this meditation. You can imagine that you are a cat, lying on the windowsill looking outside. Or a photographer or artist who wants to capture this view. Afterwards, make notes about your experience.

You can repeat the seeing meditation a few times this week. It doesn't have to be done at a window – you could look, for example, at your living room. Try to let go of all your opinions, so that instead of seeing it as 'untidy' or 'dirty', look at it as if you want to paint or draw it. You could even do so if you want! You can also look at a vase of flowers for five minutes, or the view from a bench in a park. So long as it is done without judgement and with a beginner's mind, anything will do.

Exercise 4.2: Full attention interaction

This week, interact with your child for five minutes each day with full awareness and open attention. This could be playing together, talking, or just doing something like working in the garden or cooking together. Take an uncontrolling approach during these interactions, so see what the child does and join in rather than trying to steer it yourself. If you notice the urge to steer the interaction, observe it then let it go. Remember to turn off your phone and other distractions while you do this exercise. Five minutes may seem short, but it is not uncommon to experience this exercise as quite long – simply because we aren't used to focusing on things for as long as five minutes anymore! Make notes about your experience.

Exercise 4.3: True-nature observation

Observe your child at various moments, for example while they are playing, reading, relaxing, talking or playing games. What are they especially interested in? What grabs their attention? What makes them happy? What motivates them?

Try to find moments, activities and situations that you normally wouldn't pay much attention to – the ones you look away from, and that normally take place outside your attention. Think about things you might have an aversion to (e.g. particular video games), things you think you wouldn't understand, things that might not fit with your gender typical expectations or moments when you would normally give them privacy, such as when they are alone in their room.

Exercise 4.4: Reflecting on expectations

What expectations did your parents have of you, as far as you know? Write them in your notebook. In what way have those expectations helped or hindered your development into a complete person?

What expectations do you have of your children? Write them down. What burden or pleasure do your children get from these expectations? How do they help or hinder your children's development into whole, complete individuals?

References

1   Martin, W. (1999). *The parent's Tao Te Ching: Ancient advice for modern parents*. Philadelphia, USA: Da Capo Press.

2   Brown, B. (2013). *The power of vulnerability: Teaching of authenticity, connection and courage*. Louisville, USA: Sounds True.

3   Brown, B. (2010). *The power of vulnerability*. Ted Talk. Available at: https://www.ted.com/talks/brene_brown_on_vulnerability (accessed January 2020).

4   Siegel, R. (2016). Conference: *Achtsamkeit und Mitgefühl in Therapie und Gesellschaft, Freiburg*, 23-25 Sept. Personal communication.

5   VPRO (2016). *Zomergasten in vijf minuten – Griet op den Beeck*. Available at: https://www.youtube.com/watch?v=E8e1Hl0ACQQ (accessed January 2020).

6   Campbell, J. (1990). *The hero's journey: Joseph Campbell on his life and work*. Novato, USA: New World Library.

7 Nathan DeWall, Laboratory of Social Psychology, University of Kentucky.

8 Alessandri, S. M., & Lewis, M. (1993). Parental evaluation and its relation to shame and pride in young children. *Sex Roles*, **29**, 335-343.

Chapter 5:
Rupture and repair:
Deepening the bond

'We repeat what we don't repair.'
Christine Langley-Obaugh[1]

When people care for each other and spend
much of their lives together, there are
bound to be conflicts. Siblings argue on
average once per hour; parents argue with
their teenage children once a day. When
we hear that over 40% of all marriages
in Western countries end in divorce, it's
easy to imagine just how many arguments
must take place within each and every
family home.

It's only logical that family members should argue with each other, as
everyone has their own goals that often don't align or that conflict with
each other. If a sister's morning goal is to make sure she looks nice for
school, which requires time alone in the bathroom, while her brother's goal
is to sleep as long as possible before getting ready at the last minute, then
there will be an argument if there is only one bathroom – an argument
which their parents will experience as something as trivial as locking the
bathroom door. Perhaps this is why two bathrooms is now standard for
many houses, while the average number of occupants has decreased!

I can still remember how my children, now adults, would sit close to our
small black and white television, arguing over who was allowed to see
what. Later, when we had a remote control they would argue over who
was allowed to control it. Is this why many children nowadays have a
television in their own room – simply to prevent these arguments?

Recently, I was privy to an intense argument between my two teenage
nieces. We'd had a cosy Christmas celebration with our entire extended
family, totalling more than 25 people across three generations. In the little
old-fashioned cottage in the woods (with only one bathroom!) where we
stayed, my nieces had sockets above their beds where they could charge

their phones overnight. The younger one had been given a face massager as a gift, and had put it to charge in her own socket while plugging her phone into her sister's. The argument that ensued after the older sister removed the phone from 'her' socket to charge her own took an hour and was never resolved. As their aunt, I was sleeping in the same room, and from under the covers I listened with interest to the phases of their conflict. First their mother was called to mediate, then their father, but even after the parents had left the siblings kept arguing, until both fell asleep through sheer exhaustion.

I was impressed by the parents – how they each tried to solve the conflict in their own way, how they dealt with their stress, and how they didn't undermine each other in the presence of their children (about which more in Chapter 6). I wondered if they were annoyed or embarrassed by such an overblown argument about something as simple as a plug socket. Did they feel bad about the screaming in a small house where people were trying to sleep, did they worry what the rest of the family would think of them, or were they only thinking of how spoiled their children were ('*they get presents then they act like this!*')?

Yet I also admired my nieces – how they were able to express their frustration and anger. I wondered how I might have developed differently if I could have done that as a child; if I had felt that freedom, and hadn't been afraid that a tantrum would unbalance our family by making my parents angry with me, my siblings or each other. I was even a little jealous that my nieces apparently felt sufficiently safe in the world that they could vent their frustration so shamelessly. In the end, arguments and conflicts are healthy, and the best we can do is offer a family environment in which it is safe for our children to burst out even in unreasonable anger. But to achieve that, we must work on ourselves.

An argument can feel like a rupture in a relationship, but every argument is a chance to get closer to each other and help the relationship grow. For myself, I know very well the difference between showing controlled anger to my children and flying off the handle because I'm tired, stressed or stuck in a rut. I remember clearly one occasion when I lost my composure. I'd just got divorced and took my children (then aged six and three) swimming on a nice Wednesday morning. It was a special members-only pool, located in the city centre yet planted with lots of greenery. We'd been on a waiting list for years, finally becoming members just after the divorce, and there were always friends and acquaintances there. We had a great time – picnicking on the grass, my children playing with others, sand, sun and water. I was truly savouring their enjoyment; I was so happy that we could 'still' have these moments, despite the divorce. It was as if I could feel this happiness better than ever before, and time appeared to be standing still.

When we eventually had to leave to attend to other important matters (so important that I no longer remember what they were...), my son deliberately tried to extend our stay by not getting dressed, wandering off and hiding. Meanwhile I also had to pay attention to my three year old who was running all over the place, making me constantly fret that she'd somehow end up drowning – just as my own mother used to worry about us. Wanting to prove to myself that I could manage all this without a man by my side, I wasn't about to ask anyone to look after my daughter while I got my son – I had to handle it alone.

I can't even remember how I did it, but eventually we were cycling home. I was on my bicycle, carrying all our stuff as well as my daughter on an attached seat. Meanwhile my son was on his own bike to one side of me. I was pleased to have got us away safely and on time, but also still angry and scolding my son. Suddenly, he started riding off in the wrong direction – then jumped off his bike, threw it down at the side of the road and ran away. I got off my bicycle, grabbed my daughter and ran after him screaming for all I was worth. When I finally reached him he began to cry, looked at me and said: '*Mummy, when you get that angry with me, it makes me feel worthless*'. I was silent. What a gift it was that my son could speak so clearly to make me aware of the effect of my actions on him. Here was something I had to learn, and now I had something to repair too.

Relationships between parents and children are, according to Jerry Lewis[2], the most important relationships in which people can grow – along with partner relationships and therapist-client relationships. Scientific research and clinical observation show that forming a strong emotional connection with someone important to us, and repairing disruptions of that bond when they occur, creates personal growth for both children and parents. We can keep growing throughout our lives and, to cite George Vaillant[3], '*It is fortunate that we never become too old to internalize those whom we admire*'. We become mature personalities by internalising admirable qualities from significant others – making the rules and behaviours they display part of our own identities. Forming a strong emotional bond with someone important, and repairing any ruptures caused by conflict, leads to that internalisation. The conflicts and repairs are crucial to the process.

Research on attachment used to focus on the sensitivity and adjustment of a mother towards her child, and the synchronisation of the interaction. However, when researcher Zeynep Biringen and her colleagues[4] analysed videos of mother-child interactions in microscopic detail, they discovered that only in a third of cases was the mother completely in tune with the child's emotional state. In another third the mother managed to repair her lack of adjustment by orienting herself on the reactions of her child to her own non-attuned behaviour, and in the final third the mother did not succeed in becoming attuned to her baby.

The researchers concluded that the existence of this lack of synchronisation between mother and child, and the fact that a mother can adjust herself when the baby protests, creates and strengthens the mother-child bond. Babies become desperate when their mothers don't understand them, and happy when their mothers fix this. The reparation increases the baby's trust in its mother, and also increases the baby's trust in itself – in its ability to influence the parent-child relationship. However, the researchers also concluded that the non-attuned interactions were also important, since they served to teach a child that it must sometimes be alone and to console itself.

Causing and repairing ruptures in the bond isn't just important to the early mother-baby relationship, but also to the later parent-child relationship. Guy Diamond and his research group[5] studied the effects of dramatic ruptures, such as those caused by abandonment and unresolved trauma, in relationships between adolescents and their parents. He found that such ruptures fundamentally disrupt the parent-child attachment relationship, and can lead to children trying (and often failing, sometimes with serious and even suicidal consequences) to deal with complex emotional problems by themselves.

Diamond developed an intervention called 'Attachment Based Family Therapy', to help parents and teenagers fix such ruptures. His central question for the adolescent was: *'What stopped you from asking your parent for help when you wanted to end your life?'*. This intervention proved very effective for lessening symptoms of depression and suicidal tendencies in teenagers. Parents often assume that when their children reach puberty the most important part of parenting is done, and the parent-teenager relationship is less important. This is absolutely untrue. During puberty in particular, when a child starts to push against authority and become more autonomous, a safe attachment relationship and rupture and repair of the parent bond is crucial. This is because a safe bond gives the child the confidence needed to explore the world and make mistakes, knowing that they will always be able to return to a safe harbour.

Research on interactions in partner relationships has produced similar results to that on parent-child relationships. A series of studies from John Gottman's research group[6,7] showed that the physiological stress (measured by heart rate) of both partners increases when they are in a conflict and lowers after the conflict's resolution. Contrary to what we might assume, physiological stress increases more in men than in women, even if they may show it less. Janice Kiecolt-Glaser's research group[8] reached similar conclusions by looking at the functioning of the endocrine (hormonal) and immune systems. When a conflict is unresolved, these systems become less functional – which needless to say is bad for our health! Conversely, resolving conflict can actually cause the functioning of these systems to improve.

Studies undertaken by Mark Cummings and his research team[9] have shown that conflicts between partners that are not resolved have a negative effect on children who notice them, which they do more often than parents might expect. These studies also show that whether and how much a conflict is resolved, and the explanation given by the parents about how it was or will be resolved, has a massive effect on whether and to what extent this negative effect on children is negated.

Summarizing the above paragraphs, research on both early and late parent-child relationships, as well as on interactions between partners, consistently shows the importance of normal levels of friction – and of resolving arguments afterwards. As parents, we tend not to revisit conflicts, especially when our children are happily running around afterwards. We hope and assume that they've already forgotten, and that if we don't bring it up the argument won't stick in our children's long-term memory. Unfortunately, we couldn't be more wrong. Children are masters of hiding things away and moving on, but that doesn't mean the conflict isn't still in their system. By getting uncontrollably angry, and not resolving it afterwards, we risk causing real damage to them.

Another reason why we often don't revisit conflicts is because we feel guilty about how we acted. Admitting that we were guilty of unreasonable anger towards our children is a crucial part of the restoration process, because if we can summon the courage to admit to our own mistakes – and realize that all parents make such mistakes – then we can stop isolating ourselves and connect with our children again.

When parents become unreasonably angry it's often because of stress – trouble at work, a conflict with our partner, a bad night's sleep, an impending deadline, being in a rush, concern about how our child is doing at school. All these things can cause us to 'lose it'. Unreasonable reactions can also spring from created patterns – in other words, if these kinds of conflicts have happened before, over time the participants will gradually start to exhibit the same reactions. It's as if it's a play, with each character knowing and performing their own lines.

On a deeper level, an unreasonable reaction can also be caused by our own upbringing and old traumas that we may have experienced. A father in a mindful parenting group shared how, if his son misbehaved at school, he would lose his cool and hit him. When we analyzed these situations, we discovered that his behaviour was driven by his own past at a boarding school, where he spent his entire adolescence separated from his family. At that school he was physically punished whenever he broke a rule; because of his impulsivity, this happened often. Out of fear that his equally impulsive son would suffer something similar if he misbehaved, the father repeated what had hurt him so much as a child.

Whenever we have a conflict, whether it is with a child, partner, ex-partner, boss or employee, things happen to our body – increased heartbeat, faster breathing, tensed muscles, becoming red-faced or sweating. These are all signs of stress, whereby the hormone adrenaline is released. In Chapter 3 we saw that this allows us, via the 'express route' in our brain, to very quickly prepare for 'fight or flight', a survival technique that is very important whenever we face real danger. This survival reaction also gives us a narrowed perspective, tunnel vision, and very quick judgments and reactions.

However, all this speed comes at the cost of cautious decision making and the ability to analyze situations from different angles. I once encountered an intruder in my house, in broad daylight. I was working in my front room, looked up and saw a strange man standing looking back at me. I jumped up, screaming at him – he ran away via the back door and, when I chased him into the garden, he jumped over the fence and disappeared. Not for a second did I pause to think about the wisdom of my course of action. My body reacted instantly – I was surprised I could even run that fast, and even more surprised to have scared him off. When we have a conflict with our child there is very rarely any real danger present, but our body makes us think so.

Besides the fight-or-flight reaction caused by stress, there is another factor that can stop us resolving a conflict – our ego. Anatta, the idea that the self doesn't exist, can again help with this. What makes it so hard for us to resolve a conflict by apologizing for our behaviour? Our ego resists, because we'd have to accept that we made a mistake and we are strongly attached to our own perfect self-image. We want to be model parents, and we tell ourselves we are, and admitting to ourselves and our children that we were at fault proves that image wrong. How liberating, then, is the concept of 'no-self', which helps us realize that all the stories we tell ourselves about what kind of parent (or partner, employee or friend) we are, really are no more than that – stories, our own constructions. How much easier would it be to resolve arguments if we truly believed that our 'self' doesn't exist outside our own head?

Beyond stress and ego, the very role of being a parent can get in the way of repairing a conflict. Being a parent means being a child's older and wiser guide. This can lead us to assume wrongly that we must always be wiser than our children; however, true wisdom can sometimes mean admitting that we didn't behave wisely. Maybe we struggle to say sorry to our children because we're afraid to jeopardize our parental authority and respect; but it's worth remembering that respect and authority are things we need to earn.

My daughter told me an important lesson that she learned from her teacher Mathijs van Zutphen at her sociocratic school (a free form of education based on collective decision making). A group of students was gathering wood for a campfire and didn't realize that what looked to them like a heap of loose branches was actually a 'hut' belonging to the school's youngest children. One of the youngsters became very angry when he realized what had happened to their hut. The teacher was called, listened attentively to the child's grievance, and then discussed with the students how they could restore the 'hut'. Afterwards he told them: '*If you want respect, you must give respect*'.

When repairing the bond after an argument we tend to think that, as parents, we should use it as an opportunity to educate our children, to teach them a lesson. '*I reacted too strongly, but you…*' However, the most important lesson that we can teach our children is what we've just discussed – that only after we've calmed down can we can see a situation from different perspectives, realize that nobody is perfect and every parent makes mistakes, and apologize wholeheartedly for what we've done wrong.[10] If our children can see us do that, then they will have a clear example of how to do it in their own lives. Our relationship with them is a critical blueprint for their relationships with others, and if we can't apologize for our mistakes then how can we expect them to learn to do the same?

Repairing a rupture requires understanding the feelings, intentions and desires of the other person – in other words, seeing a situation from their perspective so as to imagine what they might think, feel and want. Children learn perspective during their development, in their interactions with others. Moreover, their sense of perspective keeps developing until young adulthood, as shown by the experimental studies of Peter Fonagy's research group[11], so adolescence is an important period in the growth of this skill. Parents who can see the world from their children's perspective, and understand their feelings and needs, can in turn teach their children to understand the viewpoints and needs of others.

Perspective taking takes time. It's a *slow* process, and it requires the slower route through our brain. The 'express route' is of no use to us here; to resolve a conflict, we must use the longer route through our frontal lobe – the part of the brain that we use to understand other people's viewpoints, see situations from different angles and assess the likely consequences of our actions.

The hormone oxytocin, also called the hug- or attachment-hormone, allows us to feel empathy and compassion, connect with each other and understand someone else's point of view. Oxytocin is released when we pet animals, touch each other, smile, cuddle, fall in love and have sex – but it is also released when we meditate. While adrenaline causes us to turn away from others and trust only in our own, egotistical judgment, oxytocin does the reverse – it helps us listen to others, pay attention to their points of view and open ourselves up to their perspectives[11].

By withdrawing from situations of conflict and taking a breathing space, we can notice the stress in our body and tell ourselves: '*It's OK, let me feel it!*' And by giving ourselves self-compassion in this way, we can create the distance and space required to see our own and other people's perspectives at the same time. Only then can we reflect on our actions, apologize for any mistakes we have made, and resolve the conflict. Writer Karl Ove Knausgård[13] describes perfectly the tension between losing his cool as a parent in the heat of the moment, and seeing things from a very different perspective when the necessary distance is established.

'*As I write, I am filled with tenderness for her* [Heidi, 2 years old]. *But this is on paper. In reality, when it really counts, and she is standing there in front of me, so early in the morning that the streets outside are still and not a sound can be heard in the house, she, raring to start a new day, I, summoning the will to get to my feet, putting on yesterday's clothes and following her into the kitchen, where the promised blueberry-flavoured milk and the sugar-free muesli await her, it is not tenderness I feel, and if she goes beyond my limits, such as when she pesters and pesters me for a film, or tries to get into the room where John* [the baby] *is sleeping, in short, every time she refuses to take no for an answer but drags things out ad infinitum, it is not uncommon for my irritation to mutate into anger, and when I then speak harshly to her, and her tears flow, and she bows her head and slinks off with slumped shoulders, I feel it serves her right. Not until the evening when they are asleep and I am sitting wondering what I am really doing is there any room for the insight that she is only two years old. But by then I am on the outside looking in. Inside, I don't have a chance.*'
My Struggle. Book one. Karl Ove Knausgård

Exercises

Exercise 5.1: Walking meditation (audio track 5)

The strategy of cooling down with a 'walk around the block' when we're arguing with someone is centuries old. The walking meditation is a version of that. It is suitable for a wide range of everyday situations – from pushing the pram to the shops to walking to the printer at work – but it can be particularly helpful after an argument or any other intense interaction or problem you are faced with.

It is essential for this meditation that your mind is not focused on the goal (the supermarket, printer or resolution of the conflict), but on the walking itself. The title of John Kabat-Zinn's book *Wherever You Go, There You Are*[14] illustrates this principle beautifully. You are present at every step. The fact that you may be walking in a circle or back and forth on a short path can help with this focus – there is no goal or end point, only the journey and the act of walking.

You can do a walking meditation inside or outside. At first it may be easier to practice inside so you don't get distracted by everything that you can hear, see, feel and smell outside. It's also helpful on your first few tries to listen to the audio guide (track 5, 10 minutes long), so that you don't have to think but are led by the voice. If you walk outside, identify a route of 10 to 15 steps. You can place a branch or other object at the beginning and end if you find it helpful.

Now, walk back and forth. For the first few minutes, focus on feeling the soles of your feet touch the ground, and being aware of every step in your body. When you've settled into this, you can extend your attention from experiencing and feeling every step to awareness of your surroundings. If something catches your attention, pause and notice it then continue walking.

A walking meditation can be long or short. At mindfulness retreats, walking meditations are 45 minutes long – imagine how often you'd walk up and down your short path! Of course, you can also practice a walking meditation using a longer walk, but the essential element is that you are walking without any goal.

Exercise 5.2: Reparation in imagination

Sit down on your meditation pillow, bench or chair, and pay attention to how your body feels in this position. Make sure you're comfortable. Feel where your body makes contact with the seat, pillow or bench, and with the floor. Follow your breathing for a while with your full attention.

When you feel ready, remember an occasion when you were very angry at your child (or partner, ex-partner or someone else close to you) and which you have since felt unhappy about because, for example, you felt you reacted too strongly. Imagine the conflict as vividly as possible, as if you're experiencing it now again. Where were you? Who were you with? What did you say or do? What did other people say or do? How did you feel? What did you notice in your body? What thoughts went through your mind? What did you feel the urge to do?

When you have a vivid mental image of the situation, bring your attention to the here and now – to the present. What do you feel now, what do you notice in your body, what thoughts are around, what action impulses? Can you feel compassion for the state you are in now? Whatever you feel, say to yourself: *'It is OK, let me feel it'*. Welcome any emotion, whether it is fear, sadness, anger or hurt.

Now bring your attention to your breathing, to the movement of the air floating in and out of your body. Follow at least three breaths with your full attention, then widen your awareness to your whole body, as you sit here. Become aware of your whole, breathing body. Now, give yourself the compassion you need at this particular moment. You can put both hands on the area where your heart is, or you can embrace yourself. And you can tell yourself something like: *'This is a moment of suffering. I connect myself with all other people who are dealing with a conflict and suffering. Let me be kind to myself'*.

Now, if you feel ready, direct your attention to the person with whom you had the conflict. How do you think they feel? What thoughts might they have? What would they want? Can you allow yourself to accept what you feel, and also allow them to feel what they are feeling, whether they are angry, sad, upset or scared? Can you tell them that it is OK, whatever they feel? Can you understand things from their perspective? Can you feel compassion for the state they may be in?

What would you like to tell them, from this new level of understanding? Can you let go of your pride and truly apologize from the heart for what you did wrong, without attaching a *'But you…'*? Apologize to them in your imagination, and notice how it feels for you (perhaps vulnerable?) and for the other person.

Exercise 5.3: Reparation in practice

Whenever you have a conflict with your child, partner or others, and especially if you feel uneasy about any aspect of your behaviour, practice repairing the conflict.

First, take the time and space necessary to recover yourself and lower your stress. A walking meditation can help, or giving yourself self-compassion (see Chapter 2). Attempting to start reparation while you are still angry and stressed won't work. Sometimes three minutes of meditation will be enough to calm you down, but it can take 30 minutes, three hours or three weeks. Sometimes it can take three years before someone is ready to come back to a serious conflict!

If it helps, practice reparation in your imagination first (see Exercise 5.2) before doing it for real, and be sure not to allow yourself to add a *'but you…'*. Let go of any and all expectations about the result – this is about practicing saying sorry, letting go of your pride, and accepting that you are a human being like everyone else – a human that sometimes makes mistakes and hurts others.

Remember how important reparation is for the development of your bond with the other person. Imagine the example you'll set for your child, for instance, by being able to apologize wholeheartedly. Realize how your child's personality can grow through this repair of your relationship. Make notes about your experiences, especially about how it made you feel. If you aren't ready to apologize yet, instead make notes about what makes it so hard, and give yourself compassion.

References

1   https://www.tribuneindia.com/news/thought-for-the-day/we-repeat-what-we-don-t-repair-christine-langley-obaugh/379810.html

2   Lewis, J. M. (2000). Repairing the bond in important relationships: A dynamic for personality maturation. *American Journal of Psychiatry*, **157**, 1375-1378.

3   Vaillant G. E. (1993). *The wisdom of the ego.* Cambridge: Harvard University Press.

4   Biringen, Z., Emde R.N., & Pipp-Siegel, S. (1997). Dyssynchrony, conflict, and resolution: Positive contributions to infant development. *American Journal of Orthopsychiatry*, **67**, 4-19.

5   Diamond, G. S., Wintersteen, M. B., Brown, G. K., Diamond, G. M., Gallop, R., Shelef, K., & Levy, S. (2010). Attachment-based family therapy for adolescents with suicidal ideation: A randomized controlled trial. *Journal of the American Academy of Child and Adolescent Psychiatry*, **49**, 122-131.

6   Gottman, J.M. & Krokoff, L.J. (1989). Marital interaction and satisfaction: a longitudinal view. *Journal of Consulting and Clinical Psychology*, **57**, 47-72.

7   Gottman, J.M. (1993). A theory of marital dissolution and stability. *Journal of Family Psychology*, **7**, 57-75.

8   Kielcolt-Glaser, J., Malarkey, W.B., Chee, M.A., Newton, T., Cacioppo, J.T., Mao, H., & Glaser, R. (1993). Negative behavior during marital conflict is associated with immunological down-regulation. *Psychosomatic Medicine*, **55**, 395-409

9   Cummings, E. M., & Davies, P. T. (2002). Effects of marital conflict on children: Recent advances and emerging themes in process-oriented research. *Journal of Child Psychology and Psychiatry*, **43**, 31-63.

10 Siegel, D.J., & Hartzell, M. (2003). *Parenting from the inside out*. New York: Penguin.

11 Fonagy, P., Gergely, G., & Jurist, E. L. (Eds.). (2004). *Affect regulation, mentalization and the development of the self*. London: Karnac books.

12 Gilbert, P. (2016). *Human nature and suffering*. London: Routledge.

13 Knausgard, K. O. (2012). *My struggle. Book one*, Brooklyn: Archipelago Books.

14 Kabat-Zinn, J. (1994; 2005). *Wherever you go, there you are: Mindfulness meditation in every day life*. New York: Hachette Books.

Chapter 6:
Parenting together in good times and bad

'The nuclear family is very small. There is not enough air to breathe. When there is trouble between the father and mother, the child has no escape. That is a weakness of our time. Having a community where people can gather as brothers and sisters in the dharma, and where children have a number of uncles and aunts is a very wonderful thing.'
Thich Nhat Hanh[1]

This statement articulates beautifully the key pitfall of the nuclear family: when two parents experience problems with their relationship, the child has no one else to turn to and no escape. Nhat Hanh continues: 'Both partners in the couple should regard themselves as the gardener, the caretaker, of the other'.

Partners who help and respect each other create safe nests for their children. After all, when parents look after each other, children know that this burden will not fall on them. When children see that their parents respect each other, they too learn to respect themselves and others. And when children are confident that their parents support each other, they have the freedom to challenge them – trusting that if one parent cannot cope, the other will step in and help.

Although its principles apply to any parents, the concept of *co-parenting* is usually associated with the experience of two parents who no longer live together as a couple who collaborate to raise a child. Co-parenting, however, means parenting as a team, with the two parents deliberately and explicitly supporting rather than undermining each other in the child's presence.[2] This makes the child feel protected and safe. Mutually supportive parents help a child feel 'whole', the product of a team of two people; conversely, parents who undermine each other can damage their child's identity. Too often, parents in conflict fail to see that by supporting the relationship between the other parent and the child, they could actually also promote and improve the health of their own parent-child relationship.

Indeed, co-parents supporting and respecting each other doesn't only benefit the child. Parents themselves feel safer when supported by the co-parent. Research has shown that the quality of a co-parenting relationship has a significant impact on the quality of the individual parent-child relationships and the parenting abilities of both parents. When one parent feels supported by the other parent (and I cannot stress enough that divorced parents can do this just as well, albeit in different ways, as parents who are together), this positively influences their own parenting.

Given the impact of co-parenting quality on individual parenting ability, we are well-advised to pay attention not only to the quality of parenting we ourselves provide, but also to our relationship with the other parent(s) or caregivers. Doing so benefits everyone, but the child most of all. When parents are unhappy in their relationship, they tend either to become too close to or to withdraw from their children. Often the mother gets too close and the father backs off, but it can happen either way. Similarly, research shows that the parenting skills of parents going through a divorce can collapse temporarily, although they recover when the divorce is concluded[3]. Supportive co-parenting can protect a child against this.

As a divorced parent I've used the positive effects of supportive co-parenting many times, even at times when my ex-husband and I were barely speaking. When my teenagers came home drunk and I was worried about their alcohol intake, I told them I would discuss it with their father (and did), or said things like *'Your father and I find this behaviour unacceptable'*. Immediately I felt stronger as a single parent, because I summoned the supportive co-parent for myself and the present father for them, and I noticed how the message made more impression. When my daughter called to say she'd passed her final exams I raced home, buying flowers on the way and writing *'Congratulations!! Mum'* on the card. I then paused and put *'Dad and'* before *'Mum'*. When I gave her the flowers I saw a tear in her eye as she read *'Dad and Mum'*, and I realised how important it was to put aside any feelings of personal animosity towards my ex-husband: we were, and always will be, the father and mother of these beautiful young people!

Parents often think it's bad for their children to watch them argue. Mark Cummings has investigated the effects of parental quarrelling on children. His studies [4,5,6,7] show that while conflict itself doesn't damage children, a failure to resolve it in their presence does. The rupture-and-repair practice of the last chapter is an important tool: apologize to your partner if you've behaved badly and, if the children witnessed an argument, let them see you do it. We often think that children quickly forget conflict, but this is a fallacy. Children find it hard to ask their parents what an argument was about and whether it was resolved, perhaps through fear of burdening them, but their silence doesn't mean they don't suffer or worry.[8] Resolution from the child's point of view requires you to let go of your pride and ego and apologize sincerely to your co-parent for any aspect of your own behaviour that you're unhappy about. Do this in the presence of any child who witnessed the conflict, and make sure you don't add a *'yes, but...'*

The parents of a child should complement each other, and it's important for an individual parent to understand what the child can receive or learn better from the other parent than from themselves. For the last ten years me and my research group investigated the unique role of the father in a child's development, especially in overcoming fear and developing confidence.[9,10] Evolution has equipped fathers and mothers to be specialists in different areas of childcare: mothers are experts in the skills of care, comfort and feeding, nurturing a child's feelings and sense of empathy, while fathers specialize in challenging play and competition.

This is why some fathers perceive mothers as overprotective, while mothers may see fathers as irresponsible. If a mother lets a child beat her at a game on purpose, while the father does his best to win, then the father may feel that the mother is being 'soft' while the mother may feel that the father is just a big kid himself. Yet both parents are acting on evolutionary instinct, and the child needs both sides for healthy development. Therefore, mindful parenting means not only observing your child without judgment, but also observing the other parent and their contact with the child. This doesn't mean never judging; rather, it means postponing judgment and watching the other parent with an open mind – open to what the child needs and receives from the other parent.

Parents who feel supported by the other parent are, quite simply, better parents.[3] You can't do a complete job on your own, and you don't need to. Therefore, make sure you're supported – by asking for support, noticing it, and enlisting the support of your partner, ex-partner or other co-parents. Sharing vulnerability helps bring them on board. Talk about what you find difficult in parenting and contact with your child, what you feel apprehensive or insecure about, what you don't know, and what you can't do (yet). Be attentive to what confirmation, help or support the other parent may need from you, and make it safe for them to share what they themselves find difficult or challenging in parenting your child.

Although the Mindful Parenting group training we deliver to parents is focused not on co-parenting but on parenting style and parent-child relationships, research with trainees shows that practicing mindful parenting does positively influence the co-parenting relationship.[11] Eighty-six parents were assessed on a co-parenting scale[12] around eight weeks prior to training, just before the training began, immediately after the eight-week training period, and eight weeks later at follow-up. Our questionnaire measured both overt co-parenting (the behaviour of the parent towards the other parent when the two are together in the presence of the child) and covert co-parenting (how the parent invokes the presence of the other parent and talks about them when alone with the child). Three co-parenting dimensions were measured: the extent to which the parent encourages a sense of togetherness between the family members, the extent to which the parent undermines the other parent, and the extent to which the parents disagree and quarrel in the presence of the child. The training delivered improvements across all three dimensions, but in the disagreements and quarrels dimension most of all.

Whether or not two parents are still together in a relationship, they never truly separate because they retain a lifelong connection through their child. They will always be the parents of their child, and later perhaps grandparents to the child's own children. Nancy Bardacke, the developer of Mindfulness-Based Child Birthing and Parenting[13], has developed a beautiful meditation for expectant parents[14]. She asks the pregnant mother and her partner to sit face to face. Then she says:

'Look the person in front of you deep in the eyes. You have chosen this person to put a child on this world together. Whatever you feel about this person, now or in the future, and whatever will happen in both your lives, in your relationship, and whether you will remain together or not, this person will always be the parent of the child that is now growing and will soon see the world, and will ever be the grandparent of the children of your child to be.'

The commitment two people make when they create a child is forever. Truly seeing a co-parent, and acknowledging deeply what this commitment means for both parties, may make us feel anxious; but it can also help us to take the best possible care of the co-parent relationship in good times and bad. And, as we have shown, a healthy co-parenting relationship is good news for everyone.

Exercises

Exercise 6.1: The choiceless awareness meditation (audio track 6)

So far you have practiced a sitting meditation with attention to the breath, a bodyscan, a sitting meditation with attention to sounds and thoughts, a seeing meditation, and a walking meditation. All these meditations had a specific focus: breath, body, sounds, thoughts, images, and the sensation of walking. In the choiceless awareness meditation, which we will now introduce, there is no specific focus or 'anchor'. Instead we observe, from a distance, whatever our attention is drawn to from moment to moment. Set an alarm for ten minutes, or use audio track 6, and try to practice the meditation every day for a week.

Settle in a seated position and direct your attention first to your posture – to where your body makes contact with the floor, chair or cushion – and to your breath, until you feel reasonably comfortable and relaxed. Now let your attention go, allowing it to just float. Notice where it goes. You can make a mental note of what attracts it (e.g. sounds, an itch, plans, pain). Be aware of where your attention is, without letting it take you too far. If you feel overwhelmed you can always return to the breath or body to re-anchor yourself, and resume the meditation when you've settled again. Afterwards, make notes if you wish.

Exercise 6.2: Co-parenting observation practice

Find a moment when your co-parent is busy with your child – for example dressing them, helping with homework, cooking together, playing or putting them to bed. You can choose something that you feel your co-parent does well, or an area in which you think they are weaker or lack good judgment.

Direct your attention deliberately, in the present moment and without judgment, to how your co-parent interacts with the child and how the child responds. Notice what happens in your body while you watch, observe any thoughts and judgments that may arise (e.g. *how sweet!*; *watch out!*), and acknowledge any feelings (e.g. happiness, irritation) or action impulses (e.g. urge to leave, urge to take over) that you experience. As best you can, let go of any action impulses and continue observing. Do this for about five minutes.

If it is difficult for you to do this practice because you and your co-parent are separated and you seldom see them interact with your child, try to think of a way to organize this. Suggest for example that you could arrive earlier next time you collect your child from your co-parent (and use the time to observe interactions between them), or ask courteously if you can watch while your co-parent coaches your child's team or makes music with them. Remember, it is in everyone's best interest for you and your co-parent to have a strong co-parenting relationship.

Exercise 6.3: Co-parenting writing practice

Think about what your co-parent offers your child and write this down in your notebook.

An example might be: *'He plays guitar with her and stimulates her to read books by taking her to the library and suggesting books. He challenges her, debates with her, and lets her do things for herself that I still do for her'.*

Are you showing your co-parent how much you appreciate the unique qualities and activities that they offer your child? How do you show gratitude for it, and by doing so support your co-parent to further develop those qualities?

For example: *'I record them when they play and sing together. I tell him that I appreciate the way he helps her with her school work'.*

Think of new ways in which you might be able to support your co-parent by conveying how happy you are with what they offer to your child.

Example: *'I could say more often how much I know she learns from him. I could buy a book of songs for them to play and sing together. I could ask how he taught her to skate'.*

Exercise 6.4: Loving kindness meditation – from within to without

Loving kindness is a meditation in which you first wish yourself well, then wish your partner or other loved one well, then do the same for someone you feel mixed or negative about. Don't expect miracles: you don't need to suddenly feel loving toward an ex-partner or someone you have serious reservations about. The key is your ability to extend to another human being your unconditional good wishes and love, whoever they may be, and in so doing to develop your own compassion.

Make sure you're sitting or lying down comfortably, then close your eyes. Become aware of your body and your breath, and bring your attention to yourself. Don't think about specific things you do or don't like about yourself; instead, focus on the simple fact that you are a human being who lives, breathes, and occasionally suffers. Now, wish yourself well by saying the following sentences out loud.

Wish yourself happiness (*'May I be happy...'*)
Wish yourself peace (*'May I have peace...'*)
Wish that you may not suffer (*'May I be free of suffering...'*)

Let the sentences sink into yourself, like a stone into a well, and notice your responses. Then repeat the same sentences for the following people:

1. Your child
2. A loved one – for example a partner, family member or pet
3. Someone with whom you have had difficulties

If you prefer, you can change the sentences. The meditation simply requires three positive sentences, containing universal things that you can wish yourself and others. Other examples might be:

'May I feel safe and protected…'
'May I live with ease and kindness…'
'May I accept myself just as I am…'

If you find it difficult to wish yourself kind things, you can try seeing yourself as a vulnerable child (see Chapter 10 on schemas). Or, if it helps, you can call yourself *'Little* [your name]'. Alternatively, you could change the order of the meditation and wish kind things to your child or loved one before wishing them to yourself.

References

1   Nhat Hanh T. (1990). 'Relationships' – Community as family, parenting as a Dharma door, and the five awarenesses. *Mindfulness Bell* #3, Autumn.

2   Majdandžić, M., de Vente, W., Feinberg, M. E., Aktar, E., & Bögels, S. M. (2012). Bidirectional associations between coparenting relations and family member anxiety: A review and conceptual model. *Clinical Child and Family Psychology Review*, **15**, 28-42.

3   Bögels, S.M., Lehtonen, A., & Restifo, K. (2010) Mindful parenting in mental health care. *Mindfulness*, **1**, 107-120.

4   Cummings, E. M., Simpson, K. S., & Wilson, A. (1993). Children's responses to interadult anger as a function of information about resolution. *Developmental Psychology*, **29**, 978.

5   Cummings, E. M., Ballard, M., El-Sheikh, M., & Lake, M. (1991). Resolution and children's responses to interadult anger. *Developmental Psychology*, **27**, 462.

6   Goeke-Morey, M. C., Cummings, E. M., & Papp, L. M. (2007). Children and marital conflict resolution: Implications for emotional security and adjustment. *Journal of Family Psychology*, **21**, 744.

7   McCoy, K., Cummings, E. M., & Davies, P. T. (2009). Constructive and destructive marital conflict, emotional security and children's prosocial behavior. *Journal of Child Psychology and Psychiatry*, **50**, 270-279.

8   Diamond, G. S., & Liddle, H. A. (1999). Transforming negative parent-adolescent interactions: From impasse to dialogue. *Family Process* **38**, 5-26.

9   Bögels, S.M. & Perotti, E.C. (2011). Do fathers know best? A formal model of the paternal influence on childhood social anxiety. *Journal of Child and Family Studies*, **20**, 171-182.

10 Möller, E. L., Majdandzic, M., de Vente, W., & Bögels, S. M. (2013). The evolutionary basis of sex differences in parenting and its relationship with child anxiety in Western societies. *Journal of Experimental Psychopathology*, **4**, 88-117.

11 Bögels, S. M., Hellemans, J., van Deursen, S., Römer, M., & van der Meulen, R. (2014). Mindful parenting in mental health care: effects on parental and child psychopathology, parental stress, parenting, coparenting, and marital functioning. *Mindfulness*, **5**, 536-551.

12 Karreman, A., Van Tuijl, C., Van Aken, M. A., & Deković, M. (2008). Parenting, coparenting, and effortful control in preschoolers. *Journal of Family Psychology*, **22**, 30.

13 Bardacke, N. (2012). *Mindful birthing: Training the mind, body and heart for childbirth and beyond.* New York: Harper Collins.

14 Bardacke, N. (2012). Personal communication.

Chapter 7:
Setting boundaries:
Where I end and you begin

*'In honoring our children's sovereignty,
we make it possible for them to show
themselves in their "true seeming" and find
their own way.'*
Myla & Jon Kabat-Zinn[1]

All parents must deal with the fundamental
but difficult task of teaching their children
the laws and values needed to function in
society, while also nurturing their wish
to express themselves and develop their
unique interests and abilities. However, it
seems to be increasingly hard for today's
parents to create boundaries that teach
their children social rules. Recently, at my local greengrocer's, I saw a
young child stick his hand into the tomatoes then put one in his mouth. *'Oh
darling,'* said his mother, *'if you like tomatoes so much, we'll buy a big bag!'*

Is this mindful parenting? The mother noticed her child's liking for tomatoes,
which is good, but this would also have been a great moment to explain that
children can't grab things in shops – and definitely shouldn't eat them!

Whether it concerns tomatoes or anything else, parents must teach their
children society's rules (assuming they agree with them), and help them
deal with the frustration that these rules can cause. If the mother in my
example had told her son: *'These tomatoes are for buying, not eating!'*, and
had paid for a small bag without giving any to the child, then the child
might have felt ashamed and become angry at his mother. Having to deal
with the shame and embarrassment of breaking a rule and being publicly
corrected, as well as with frustration and anger at not getting what they
want, is an important developmental lesson for children.

Why did the mother keep this lesson from her son? It probably has to do
with *parental experiential avoidance*: the mother was trying to protect the
child from feelings of shame or anger. Why, we can only guess; there are

many possibilities. It may be that this mother's own experiences have made it hard for her to enforce boundaries, or that she fears other people thinking her a bad parent if her son doesn't get what he wants. Perhaps she suffers from social anxiety and worries that her son will develop similar problems, or perhaps she had an abusive father and fears aggression even from her own child. Possibly she just adores her child and thinks he can do no wrong, or she thinks being a loving parent means avoiding any ruptures in their relationship. Or perhaps she's just exhausted because the boy has already had several tantrums that morning and she doesn't feel ready for another one! Whatever the reason, she has missed an opportunity to teach her child an important lesson.

When I was young, creativity was an important value in our household. Every home we lived in had a built-in studio where my mother would work, but where we children were also welcome to draw, paint, press, weave or sew. All the material was available to us and our friends. We were never warned not to make a mess, yet we would always clean up after ourselves. I have so many great memories of wonderful hours spent playing and working in the studio, with my mother's classical music playing in the background. I remember how the behaviour of a friend, who impulsively emptied an entire tube of paint or ran off when it was time to clean up, would shock me – the values of being careful with materials that we could always use but never waste, and of leaving things as clean as we found them, were so central to our upbringing that they were 'internalized'.

Besides that, I will always remember the deep attention that my mother had for these creative moments – her presence, availability, time, tranquility and patience to help us and to do things for us, and her sincere interest in what we created. For all five of her children she made scrapbooks, keeping track of our drawing skills from early childhood to the end of adolescence, with each drawing including a date, notes and often the title we chose. These scrapbooks are unique records of our cognitive, creative and psychological development – of our dreams, interests, fears and fascinations. I might even consider the combination of space for creativity with clear values and boundaries to be the most important part of my upbringing. I often wonder how much time today's children spend drawing, painting, crafting and sewing, now that televisions and computers have become such a central part of our life, and what they might be missing.

When bringing up my own children I sometimes found the setting of boundaries quite challenging. When my kids decided to make yet another den and pulled all the blankets off the beds, making a mess that they couldn't or wouldn't clean up themselves, I always wanted to let them – because I saw how much fun they had and how creative the stories they invented were. It was only when I took a moment to consider my own well-being that I conceded that sometimes I would really rather they didn't – because I lacked the energy to clean up after them or it was so late that they wouldn't have time to play properly. So I implemented a new rule that they should always ask permission before making a den – then I would take time to consider not only with whether it fitted with other plans for the day but also with how I felt.

I also learned that it is best not to say '*no*' too often, and always to pause and decide whether a particular '*no*' is worth sticking to even if it causes disappointment or a tantrum. Sometimes, doing this turns a '*no*' into a wholehearted '*yes*'. Once, I went to the outside terrace where my son and daughter were sitting at a table painting on big pieces of paper. My daughter had filled her page and was happily continuing her art on the white terrace wall that the table stood against. My first instinct was to rush over and stop her; however, I decided to watch her paint for a bit longer, and then I offered that they could paint the whole wall if they wanted! They went to fetch all their friends living in the same street, and for the rest of the day a group of children painted my terrace wall, some even standing on a ladder. For years afterwards I kept enjoying that wall!

Limiting children is important for their socialization, and psychology researchers have explored the effects of setting adequate boundaries. In a typical study[2], the parent and child are asked to wait in a room that is empty except for a brightly coloured xylophone. The parent has previously been instructed to do whatever they would normally do at home to prevent the child from touching the object or playing with it. Parents who set mindful boundaries appear to be clear about the boundary, in that they use clear verbal and bodily indications to communicate it to the child. They help them accept it by distracting them and explaining it to them, and they show empathy for the child's desires and developing self-control.

We know from a series of psychological studies that growing up with parents who set appropriate boundaries generally leads to more socially acceptable behaviour, better school performance, less aggression, fewer antisocial behavioural problems, fewer internalized symptoms such as fear and depression, and better focus, emotion regulation and self-control[3,4]. Some studies have found that the positive effects of parental limit-setting continue until much later in a child's development[5]. We also know that parents who set clear boundaries tend to be warmer towards their children, and to encourage them to be more autonomous.

Conversely, research has also shown that strict or inappropriate boundaries can lessen the intrinsic motivation and creativity of children. Creative architects, for example, report that as children they were generally given a great deal of freedom by their parents[6]. The Israeli schoolteacher and psychotherapist Haim Ginott[7] has said that boundaries, when they are necessary, should be explained in a concise, impersonal and informative way – for example *'Walls are not for painting'* rather than *'You are not allowed to paint on walls'*.

Richard Koestner and his colleagues[8] conducted an experiment to find out whether it mattered how children are limited. They asked 44 six and seven year olds to paint their dream house in ten minutes. These were their instructions:

> *'I'm interested in seeing how children paint, so I want you to paint a picture. Please paint a house that you'd like to live in. You can create whatever kind of house you'd like and add whatever you like to the painting. You might want to give your house a garden with trees and animals, for example. It can be as imaginative as you like.'*

The children were either given 'controlling' boundaries, 'informative' boundaries or no boundaries at all. The informative boundary group were told:

> *'Before you begin, I'd like to tell you a few things about the way we paint here. I know that sometimes it's fun just to mess around with paint, but here we need to keep the materials and space clean for other children who will need to use them. The smaller sheet of paper is for you to paint on, and the big one is a boundary to keep the table clean. The paint also needs to be kept clean, so your brush will need to be washed and wiped on a paper towel before you change color. I know some children don't always like being neat, but here it is necessary to work cleanly.'*

For the controlling boundary group, the added instructions were as follows:

> *'Before you begin, I'd like to tell you a few things you'll have to do. These are the rules we have here for painting. You must keep the paint clean. You can only paint on this small sheet of paper, so don't spill paint on the bigger sheet. And wash and wipe your brush on a paper tissue before switching colors, so the colors don't get all mixed up. I want you to be a good boy/girl and not to make a mess of the paint.'*

After the experiment, the children were allowed to choose between painting another picture (of whatever they liked) or doing a jigsaw puzzle. Afterwards, they were asked how much fun they'd had painting. Then their dream house paintings were judged based on creativity and technical quality, as well as on the use of colour and elaboration, by experts and students who knew nothing of the conditions under which the paintings had been created.

The researchers found that the children who were given controlling boundaries enjoyed the painting exercise less, and were also less motivated to continue (they chose the puzzle more often, and if they did continue painting they did it for a shorter time). Their dream house paintings were less creative, less developed, had less colour and were of a lesser technical quality. The groups with informative boundaries and no boundaries at all did better across the board than the group with controlling boundaries. On some aspects (such as technical quality) there was no difference between the informative boundary group and the group with no boundaries; however on others (such as creativity) the group without boundaries did best of all.

This study shows that my mother intuitively did the right thing by giving her children space when it came to our creative development. But it also shows that when it is necessary to set and enforce boundaries, it matters greatly how you do it. You should explain in an informative way why the boundaries are necessary, and acknowledge the natural desire of the child to experiment without limits.

Setting boundaries for our children begins with recognizing our own limits. The psychotherapist and parenting coach Debbie Pincus describes this beautifully as *'the line you draw around yourself to show where you end and where your child begins'*. Meditating in the lotus position, you can imagine placing a rope or drawing a line around yourself to define your boundary. You can also imagine your silhouette and feel your skin – the boundary of your body. This can be particularly helpful for those who have suffered abuse – whose boundaries were not respected sexually, physically or mentally. Feel the physical boundaries of your body and tell yourself: *'this is my body, my body belongs to me'*.[9]

Yoga or mindful movement is a great way to become aware of your physical boundaries (see Exercise 7.1). By listening to your body, you can feel physically where a specific boundary is at that moment – for example how far can you stretch your leg before it hurts? And you can do the same thing mentally – by taking some time to sit silently, you can avoid getting lost in the rush of ongoing contact with your children and others. Regularly taking a breathing space to 'check in' with yourself helps you become aware of how you're doing (your physical and mental state), and of your mental and emotional boundaries at that moment.

It is important for you to feel and define these boundaries for yourself, and to accept that you now have them. For example, it may be that one day you're fine with your children building a den, but the next day you don't have the capacity to help and cope with it. Feeling, defining and accepting makes it easier to communicate these boundaries in an informative rather than controlling way, and to respond with equanimity to your child's reaction to these boundaries.

A child grows inside its mother, and with the cutting of the umbilical cord the first step towards independence is taken – their bodies have been separated and a boundary where mother ends and child begins has been defined. By being aware of your own boundaries, and making them clear to your children, you can help them on their journey towards independence. They will discover that parent and child aren't one and the same, but different beings – each with their own needs and boundaries. Your children grow in autonomy when they say no to you and realize that you hear and accept their view. A child who says he is full and has this view accepted will trust himself to know when he's had enough to eat. In the same way, your child's autonomy can grow by learning about your boundaries – because you feel them, explain them in an informative way, give him the freedom to oppose them, but ask that they accept them if they are important enough to you.

Setting boundaries also involves our own resources. Evolutionary psychologists see maternity as conditional – nature prepares mothers to take care of their children, but they also have the option to delegate that care to another. Positive emotions such as love and attachment help parents to engage with the investment they have made in offspring; conversely, outbursts of anger or disinterest may be a sign that it is time to direct internal resources towards something else. Emotions such as guilt or shame (see Chapter 8) can suppress or adjust such anger and disinterest. According to evolutionary psychologists, a couple will negotiate over the amount of care that each of them gives the child, with each parent trying to minimize their own contribution and maximize the other's[10]. In this negotiation, it is also important who is relatively better at a task (*comparative advantage*) – for example, it is obviously the case that mothers are better at breastfeeding than fathers.

Becoming aware of your boundaries is about protecting and reserving your own resources, and can help prevent you from falling into reactive parenting. When we exhaust our resources without recharging them, it can result in sudden outbursts of anger or lapses into indifference (a version of the fight or flight response). This can have an impact on our children, but also on our partners, other parents and any other people involved with our children.

If we arrive home tired and feel disappointed because our partner hasn't cleaned the house, cooked dinner or got the children started on their homework, do we generally pause to feel our boundaries, discuss them constructively with our partner and ask if they can possibly do the jobs now? Unlikely! Too often we get angry, scold the children because they haven't met our unspoken (and often unreasonable) expectations, or argue with our partner. This happens because we have exhausted our resources, and are reacting on instinct alone.

To avoid exhausting your resources, become aware of where your boundaries are and when you need time to recharge. Take a breathing space, pay attention to how you're doing, then ask yourself what you need at this moment.

Exercises

Exercise 7.1: Yoga or mindful movement (audio track 7)

Yoga or mindful movement practices are an excellent way to identify the boundaries of your body. It is not about pushing yourself to achieve and stretch as far as possible, but rather to gauge precisely how a position feels for you and where your boundary is right now. You can find the limit, hold it while breathing in and out, then test whether or not you are able to go any further.

Try to do a 10 minute mindful movement practice every day this week (track 7), or choose other yoga or mindful movement practices that help you to consciously feel and respect your physical limits. To quote my beach yoga teacher Wytske Hoekstra, 'Listen to the wisdom of your own body more than to my voice'.

Make notes about your experiences if you wish.

Exercise 7.2: Feeling limits

In situations when you aren't able to feel your limits well, or if you find that you've gone beyond your limits, take time out for a breathing space. Sit down, notice your breathing, and remind yourself that if you can't feel your limits well then you risk going beyond them with negative consequences for others.

Think about what kind of situations these might be – perhaps when you do jobs that you feel your child or partner should do, when you give in to others' wishes when you'd personally prefer something else, or when your give your children so much time and help that you have no time left for your own work or relaxation.

After the breathing space, see if you want to do or say something.

Exercise 7.3: Imagining limits

Sit on your meditation cushion, bench or chair, and take a few minutes to feel the contact between your body and what you're sitting on. Become aware of your posture and your breath. Now let a situation come to the surface where your child (or partner, or someone else) crossed your limits and you let this happen. It can be an isolated incident, or something that happens regularly.

Some examples: your toddler continued to demand attention after you made it clear that he shouldn't disturb you; your child never cleans up after making a mess; your teenager came home very late without letting you know after you'd agreed in advance that she would send a message; your partner always reads the newspaper over dinner even though you've asked him several times not to.

Imagine the situation or problem as vividly as possible, then think about the following questions. What made you notice that your limits had been crossed? What did you feel in your body? What makes it difficult to communicate and enforce your limit? Do you see any connection with how you were brought up?

Now that you're aware of how it feels for you when a limit is reached, and of what you find difficult about setting, communicating and enforcing limits, what will you do differently in future? Try this out in your imagination and see how it feels. Write down what you think you might do.

Here's an example from a parent in a mindful parenting training group:

'My partner reads the newspaper during family dinners, even though I've asked him not to because I feel it's important for us to have time to talk with our daughter. I feel when my limit is crossed because all my energy disappears. I feel sad, alone, and worry about how this is for my son. I find it difficult to stick to my limit because I think my partner is stressed about work and he needs to read during dinner to unwind. I'm also afraid that he will get angry at me, and that our daughter will be scared if we argue. My father was always absent during dinner, which made me feel ignored by him as a child. My mother never complained to my father about his absence. Now I realize that I want to talk about this with my partner in order to explain how I feel when he reads the newspaper, how I felt during childhood dinners when my own father was absent, and what I need for myself and for our family.'

References

1   Kabat-Zinn, M. & Kabat-Zinn, J. (1998; 2014) *Everyday blessings: The inner work of mindful parenting*. New York: Hachette Books.

2   Lengua, L. J., Honorado, E., & Bush, N. R. (2007). Contextual risk and parenting as predictors of effortful control and social competence in preschool children. *Journal of Applied Developmental Psychology*, **28**, 40-55.

3   Mattanah, J. F. (2001). Parental psychological autonomy and children's academic competence and behavioral adjustment in late childhood: More than just limit-setting and warmth. *Merrill-Palmer Quarterly*, **47**, 355-376.

4   Schroeder, V. M., & Kelley, M. L. (2010). Family environment and parent-child relationships as related to executive functioning in children. *Early Child Development and Care*, **180**, 1285-1298.

5   Denham, S. A., Workman, E., Cole, P. M., Weissbrod, C., Kendziora, K. T., & Zahn-Waxler, C. (2000). Prediction of externalizing behavior problems from early to middle childhood: The role of parental socialization and emotion expression. *Development and Psychopathology*, **12**, 23-45.

6   MacKinnon, D. W. (1962). The nature and nurture of creative talent. *American Psychologist*, **17**, 484.

7   Ginott, H. G. (1959). The theory and practice of 'therapeutic intervention' in child treatment. *Journal of Consulting Psychology*, **23**, 160-166.

8   Koestner, R., Ryan, R. M., Bernieri, F., & Holt, K. (1984). Setting limits on children's behavior: The differential effects of controlling vs. informational styles on intrinsic motivation and creativity. *Journal of Personality*, **52**, 233-248.

9   Levy, T.M. & Orlans, M. (2014). *Attachment, trauma and healing: Understanding and treating attachment disorders in children, families and adults*. London and Philadelphia: Jessica Kingsley Publishers.

10 Bögels, S.M. & Perotti, E.C. (2011). Do fathers know best? A formal model of the paternal influence on childhood social anxiety. *Journal of Child and Family Studies*, **20**, 171-182.

Chapter 8:
Guilt and shame: Forgiving, connecting, apologizing

'He showed the words "chocolate cake" to a group of Americans and recorded their word associations. "Guilt" was the top response. If that strikes you as unexceptional, consider the response of French eaters to the same prompt: "celebration".'
Michael Pollan[1]

Despite their ceaseless efforts on behalf of their children, many parents struggle with guilt. My mother would always rush home at the end of a working day, and as a child I couldn't understand her haste. Now I have children of my own, I do understand. It was the guilt of a working mother – the sense that it's wrong to need or want to work, because a mother (and a Dutch mother especially!) should be with her children. It is with this same feeling of guilt that Dutch mothers take their children to the crèche each morning and pick them up at the end of the day.

Just as the words 'chocolate cake' don't cause dietary guilt in every culture, so using a crèche or letting a child be cared for by a nanny doesn't cause parental guilt in every culture. In any case, that particular source of potential guilt vanishes when a child starts school, because then we're following society's rules rather than our own. Nevertheless, parents still struggle with guilt of all kinds. They may feel guilty because their marriage ended in divorce, their children seem to be constantly packing and unpacking bags, and they are growing up in a 'broken home'. They may feel guilty because they only had one child, and he or she is missing out on the experience of growing up with siblings. Or perhaps they feel guilty each time they see the scar where their child fell down the stairs while they were arguing, or whenever they think of the period of depression that caused them to miss an important part of their child's development.

After the early years of motherhood, when I'd been too busy for any serious sport, I decided to play a tennis tournament again for the first time, while my young daughter went to a junior athletics competition with her older stepsister. Playing a game with her sister, she didn't notice a metal post and lost three-quarters of both her new front teeth. For years after that I didn't play tennis, because I felt that if I'd only gone to the athletics competition instead of my tournament, it wouldn't have happened and she would still have her teeth. This phenomenon is called *hindsight bias* – if we'd known ahead of time what would happen, we would have done something else.

Parents tend to feel guilty about their child's problems, even if they are outside their control. Mothers of children with hemophilia, a rare genetic disorder where bleeding occurs in the muscles and joints because of a lack of clotting factors (proteins required for blood coagulation), have been discovered to have not only more parental stress, but also more parental guilt and shame[2]. The same is true for mothers of children who harm themselves (for example cutting)[3], mothers of autistic children[4] (even though we know that in the majority of cases autism is caused by genetics), children with 'difficult' temperaments[5], and children who have trouble sleeping[6].

In the documentary *Wrong Time, Wrong Place*[7] about the mass shooting of 69 people on a summer youth camp on the Norwegian island of Utøya in 2011, the Russian parents of one of the victims talked about feeling guilty that they hadn't given their daughter swimming lessons when she was young. She was shot dead at the water's edge. Parental guilt is often irrational or exaggerated – it is clear to us as viewers that the parents were in no way to blame for the death of their daughter, but this doesn't change the way they feel themselves.

Mothers suffer more from parental guilt than fathers[8]. A psychological research study asked Finnish mothers to write about maternal emotions that they found difficult or felt were prohibited. Their pieces showed that maternal guilt is caused partly by the mother and child having different goals and negotiating over them, but also by the 'motherhood myth'[9] – the idea that good mothers should invest constant, intensive and high-quality time and effort on behalf of their children.

Is parental guilt useful? Guilt cannot exist without empathy, and empathy is essential for good parenting. Guilt generally springs from unjust or bad behaviour (in Buddhism people speak of 'right action') and it is connected with how others are affected by behaviour. Parental guilt can be seen as a guardian, protecting both parent and child against parental aggression, negligence and preferential treatment of one child over another. No matter how often I left my umbrella on the train or at a bus stop, it never happened with my babies. Parental guilt helps us to stay constantly alert while our child is still fragile and dependent.

Guilt is a warning not to follow an impulse – don't eat that chocolate, don't lose your temper with your child, don't stay at that party when your children need you at home. However, it also functions as a self-punishment if we do follow an impulse – eaten the chocolate, lost temper with child, stayed too long at the party. It has long been known that punishment is a poor way to change behaviour, and rewarding appropriate behaviour is a far quicker and less painful way to achieve a result. So I stay too long at the party – what will my children do? Eat chips, drink cola, spend too long on their computer, go to bed late? How bad does that seem to them?! Better savour the good time I had on the party, the good time they had being free at home, and tomorrow savour the time we'll have together as a family!

Self-punishment due to guilt is also unhelpful for our parenting. If we blame ourselves for not doing things better, then we'll tend to do the same with people around us such as our partners and children. Even if we manage to avoid criticizing or punishing others in this way, our children will witness and internalize our own self-punishing behaviour. And, over time, how we treat ourselves will become their working model for how they should treat themselves.

Guilt about the effects of our choices on our children can have another unwanted side effect – compensational behaviour. Parents who feel guilty may begin spoiling their children or taking over some of their responsibilities in order to 'make up for it' – and to make themselves feel better, of course. Needless to say, these tactics will ultimately help neither the parent nor the child.

Feelings of guilt about mistakes we've made as parents can help us to take positive action, however. Most obviously, we can admit to ourselves that we feel a level of guilt proportional to the offence, apologize, and repair the damage[10]. Our behaviour has consequences, and in parenting situations we can take responsibility for them by talking it over with our child, apologizing for the pain we've caused (see Chapter 5 about conflicts and reparation), and if appropriate asking for forgiveness. If we can view our mistakes with self-compassion, put ourselves in a vulnerable position and forgive ourselves, then we'll be much better placed to learn from our mistakes than if we punish or isolate ourselves.

Whether you were mostly to blame in a particular situation or not, working through the guilt with meditation, a conversation (or written letter) and self-forgiveness frees you of inhibition and makes the bond open and free again. This is possible even long after the fact, as shown by the Dutch book *Leven en dood van een dertienjarige*[11] ('Life and Death of a Thirteen Year Old'). In this moving account, a father writes a letter to his daughter decades after she took her own life at the age of 13. He doesn't write about any wider factors such as the girl's mother (his ex-wife) or her teachers, social workers, classmates and friends. Instead, he explores the signals he missed and how this happened, admits his guilt, and asks for forgiveness both from his daughter and himself.

We know less about the role of shame in parenting than we do about guilt. We feel ashamed if our child behaves badly because we experience 'shared identity' – when we become parents, our image of ourselves becomes partly informed by who our child is and how we feel we're doing as parents[12]. As a result we tend to place high importance on what others think of our children; we feel ashamed if our child is perceived as unattractive, bad-mannered or unruly, or if the family unit ceases to function smoothly. Yet the majority of us are barely aware of how such shame can itself influence us and, like anger, lead to reactive parenting.

In my lab we researched the role of 'Fear of Negative Child Evaluation' on the transmission of social anxiety from parents to children[13]. We researched more than a hundred young couples having their first child, from pregnancy onward. When their baby was four months old, both parents completed a questionnaire about how afraid they were of their child being evaluated negatively by others. Parents who tended to worry about what others thought of them also tended to worry about what people thought of their baby. This fear of negative evaluation not only points to possible future anxiety problems for the child; it also suggests that the parents may raise their child in an insular and overprotective way. It's somewhat understandable when the parents of a screaming toddler or moody teenager worry what others may think of their child; however there is clearly no rational reason to think that anyone will disapprove of a four-month old baby.

When children are different from others, for example because they have a physical difference such as a cleft lip, a mental health diagnosis such as ADHD, autism or an anxiety disorder, or even just particularly high or low intelligence, shame can severely obstruct the parent in doing what is best for their child. Instead of researching the child's problem and understanding what they might require in order to function optimally, parents often start to worry about what others will think of their child, and fall back into reactive and negative styles of parenting in order to make their child meet the expectations that they (wrongly) perceive in others.

Although reasonable and realistic levels of guilt can have a positive effect on parental behaviour, shame always affects parenting negatively. This is because guilt provokes a desire to invest in the child – to apologize, repair the damage and reconnect. Shame, though, causes us to isolate ourselves from the event that caused it. So when our child does something that makes us feel ashamed, we tend to distance ourselves from our child[14] and also from any other people who may be aware of the shaming event.

Shame can also lead to antagonistic anger and regret, and thus cause reactive parenting[15]. Marchelle Scarnier and her colleagues[16] researched the effect of guilt and shame on parenting. They asked 93 parents to try to recall the worst behaviour their child ever exhibited between the ages of three and 18. It could be a one-off event, or a behaviour that the child showed more often. The parents were asked to write down the events that transpired. Their accounts often included factors such as physical or verbal aggression, outbursts of anger, alcohol use, sex, running away, lying, stealing, breaking things, poor grades, not doing homework and so on. The parents were then asked to describe how they felt in that moment, and how they reacted. Shame and guilt were both associated with a desire to repair the damage caused by the child, but only shame was associated with avoidance behaviour – a desire to withdraw from others, and for the ground to swallow up both parent and child.

In a second experiment, the researchers asked parents to imagine a scene where their child hit a neighbour's child while they were playing together, and while the neighbour was watching. Again, feelings of guilt were connected with attempting to repair the damage (in this case by adequate disciplining of the child), but shame and anger were linked to overreactive parenting. We can therefore see that guilt is more healthy and functional than shame in helping parents to modify their child's behaviour in an appropriate, healthy and constructive manner.

Mindful parenting involves a constantly renewing awareness of what emotions are triggered by the behaviour of our child and our role as a parent. It's about how parenting *feels*. By taking a three-minute breathing space if our child misbehaves, or practicing fuller meditations when considering more significant parenting issues and plans, we gain insight into our own emotions and can prevent reactive parenting. To achieve this, though, it's important to realize that we're all susceptible to parental experiential avoidance – the tendency to avoid any negative emotions our child may trigger in in us – which can often lead to reactive parenting. By learning how to 'be' with negative emotions triggered by contact with our child, including feelings of guilt and shame that may sometimes arise, and noticing and regulating the effects of these emotions on our behaviour, we can all learn to become the parent we want to be.

Exercises

Exercise 8.1: Setting your own meditation program

In the preceding chapters we've discussed many types of meditation: breathing, bodyscan, sounds, thoughts, breathing space, seeing, walking, choiceless awareness, self-compassion, loving kindness and mindful moving.

What meditation or combination of meditations do you want to practice this week? Make a plan, including details of how long and how often you will meditate.

Exercise 8.2: Guilt, shame and reparation

Is there something you feel ashamed and/or guilty about as a parent? It can be big or small. How does this shame or guilt influence you, positively or negatively, and how do you think it might influence your parenting? Is it helpful or unhelpful? Is there something you want to apologize for and/or something you would like to repair relating to feelings of guilt or shame? Make notes on this, or meditate over it.

Take your time before beginning any potential reparative action – talk about it with your partner or friends, for example. A carefully thought through reparation will have a much more positive impact on a relationship than a quick reaction. Maybe you need first to forgive yourself for what you did wrong, perhaps by writing yourself a compassionate letter. If you feel ashamed, consider whether there may be other parents experiencing similar emotions and relate yourself to them. Give yourself compassion, for example by putting your hand on your heart.

References

1   Pollan, M. (2009). *In defense of food: An eater's manifesto*. London: Penguin Books.

2   Kim, W. O., Kang, H. S., Cho, K. J., Song, Y. A., & Ji, E. S. (2008). Comparative study on parenting stress, guilt, parenting attitude, and parenting satisfaction between mothers with a hemophilic child and a healthy child. *Korean Journal of Women Health Nursing*, **14**, 270-277.

3   McDonald, G., O'Brien, L., & Jackson, D. (2007). Guilt and shame: experiences of parents of self-harming adolescents. *Journal of Child Health Care*, **11**, 298-310.

4   Meirsschaut, M., Roeyers, H., & Warreyn, P. (2010). Parenting in families with a child with autism spectrum disorder and a typically developing child: Mothers' experiences and cognitions. *Research in Autism Spectrum Disorders*, **4**, 661-669.

5   McBride, B. A., Schoppe, S. J., & Rane, T. R. (2002). Child characteristics, parenting stress, and parental involvement: Fathers versus mothers. *Journal of Marriage and Family*, **64**, 998-1011.

6   Schaeffer, C. E. (1990). Night waking and temperament in early childhood. *Psychological Reports*, **67,** 192-194.

7   Appel, J. (2012). *Wrong time, wrong place*. IDFA opening documentary, Amsterdam, 2012.

8   Harvey, O. J., Gore, E. J., Frank, H., & Batres, A. R. (1997). Relationship of shame and guilt to gender and parenting practices. *Personality and Individual Differences*, **23**, 135-146.

9   Rotkirch, A., & Janhunen, K. (2010). Maternal guilt. *Evolutionary Psychology*, **8**, 90-106.

10 Tangney, J. P., Miller, R. S., Flicker, L., & Barlow, D. B. (1996). Are shame, guilt, and embarrassment distinct emotions? *Journal of Personality and Social Psychology*, **70**, 1256-1269.

11 Sanders, A. & Diekstra, R. (2016). *Leven en dood van een dertienjarige: 'Het is net alsof ik hier niet hoor...'* [Life and death of a 13-year-old: 'It's just as if I don't belong here..']. Amsterdam: Prometheus.

12 Aron, A., Aron, E. N., Tudor, M., & Nelson, G. (1991). Close relationships as including other in the self. *Journal of Personality and Social Psychology*, **60**, 241-253.

13 de Vente, W., Majdandzic, M., Colonnesi, C., & Bögels, S. M. (2011). Intergenerational transmission of social anxiety: the role of paternal and maternal fear of negative child evaluation and parenting behaviour. *Journal of Experimental Psychopathology*, **2**, 509-530.

14 Lickel, B., Schmader, T., Curtis, M., Scarnier, M., & Ames, D.R. (2005). Vicarious shame and guilt. *Group Processes and Intergroup Relations*, **8**, 145-157.

15 Tangney, J. P., Wagner, P., Fletcher, C. & Gramzow, R. (1992). Shamed into anger? The relation of shame and guilt to anger and self-reported aggression. *Journal of Personality & Social Psychology*, **62**, 669-675.

16 Scarnier, M., Schmader, T., & Lickel, B. (2009). Parental shame and guilt: Distinguishing emotional responses to a child's wrongdoings. *Personal Relationships*, **16**, 205-220.

Chapter 9:
Love is blind: Denial
and acceptance

*'One of the most satisfying feelings I know –
and also one of the most growth-promoting
experiences for the other person – comes from
my appreciating this individual in the same
way that I appreciate a sunset. People are
just as wonderful as sunsets if I can let them
be. In fact, perhaps the reason we can truly
appreciate a sunset is that we cannot control
it. When I look at a sunset as I did the other
evening, I don't find myself saying, "Soften
the orange a little on the right hand corner,
and put a bit more purple along the base,
and use a little more pink in the cloud color.
I don't do that. I don't try to control a sunset.
I watch it with awe as it unfolds".'*
Carl Rogers[1]

If a baby is unfortunate enough to be born blind, its parents will go through
a mourning process for what they, the child and their family will miss, and
the fact that their home and lives will need to adapt significantly to the
child's disability. Later, if the blind child bumps into something, the parents
won't yell *'Look where you're going!'* because they know the child can't see.
Sadly, the same does not hold true for all conditions.

If a child has a less visible difference, such as ADHD, he or she may still
be scolded for not thinking things through, paying attention or sitting still
– even though these are difficult skills for children with ADHD. In the
same way it is futile to tell a child with autism to adjust, to think about
others or to play along with games, because these are specific challenges
for autistic children.

Accepting a child's inevitable imperfections, which may include a
recognizable disability or may simply be their own unique set of qualities
and differences, requires first that we mourn for what the child can't do or
won't be – what they and we may lose, what the parent-child relationship

can never be, and the kind of family we must become. Only after this acceptance has taken place can we truly perceive the specific nature, abilities and needs of our individual child, and help them to live as rich, meaningful and fulfilling a life as possible.

Professor Lynn Murray told me about research she'd done with children born with a cleft lip[2]. A major challenge when conducting research is that it's unethical to withhold things that children need, such as parental attention, or to expose them to damaging experiences such as parental stress solely in order to investigate their long-term impact on development. Because of this we still don't know, for example, the long-term effects of methylphenidates such as Ritalin on children with ADHD (a medication currently used by around 5% of children in developed countries) – because in order to explore that scientifically we'd need to draw lots to decide whether or not a child gets the pills and check back on them half a lifetime later.

Leaving any individual child without a potentially helpful and effective treatment just for research purposes is clearly unethical. Yet if we were simply to follow two natural groupings of children with ADHD, one taking medication and one refusing it, we are outside laboratory conditions and can never know for sure if any differences that develop could be explained by other variables. Parents who do and do not choose that their child will use such medications may vary in other ways: they may have different expectations of their child, eat more healthily, move home more often, have difficulty accepting the child's diagnosis or any number of other potential factors.

As a consequence of this issue, natural experiments have emerged as a useful alternative to scientifically designed experiments. With natural experiments, real life is used as a randomizing factor to create two separate groups with similar qualities. In Murrey's research, four hospitals were used – A and B, where babies with a cleft lip were operated on shortly after birth, and C and D where the same operation was performed three or four months later. The hospitals were located in broadly similar areas, and which one parents used depended largely on where they lived, so the placement into groups was ultimately quite random.

Murrey researched how the mother-child relationship developed in the early and later surgery groups. Mothers whose babies were operated on soon after birth paid closer attention when looking at their child, and were more sensitive and positively involved with their child than the mothers whose children received the operation later. These latter mothers tended to look away from their child, and were less sensitive to the baby's signals. When the babies were two months old, the children with later surgery looked at their mothers less and were more stressed. Assessed at 18 months, those with early surgery were cognitively more advanced than those whose operations had been performed later.

This difference was explained by the children with later surgery having received less sensitivity and positive involvement from their mothers, and particularly by their having been looked at less. Looking away is a metaphor for not accepting the child's disability – the mother doesn't want to see it because it is too painful – but it comes at the cost of giving the baby the attention it needs. This lack of attention damages the quality of the mother-child bond, and may eventually damage the child's own perception of themselves and their self-worth. In Murrey's project the solution was clear – an early operation is preferable for babies born with a cleft lip – but for other forms of difference the solution may be less simple. What is always certain is that looking away is never the answer!

Literal or metaphorical looking away from the imperfections of a child is driven, again, by our concept of *parental experiential avoidance*[3], which we'll explore in more detail. We all have a tendency to push away negative emotions such as guilt, shame, sadness, fear, pain, anger, jealousy and boredom, simply because we don't want to feel them. Meanwhile we try to cling onto positive emotions such as happiness, love, enjoyment and bliss. According to Buddhism, this is the cause of much of our suffering – holding on too tightly to what we enjoy, and trying too hard to avoid what we dislike.

Why do real flowers seem so much more beautiful to us than fake ones? It's at least partly because we know that living flowers will soon wither and die, and this knowledge makes us enjoy them more. They're temporary – we can't keep them forever, and we'll need to let them go. The Zen sentence '*this too will pass*' is always a great source of consolation to me, no matter where I am. A work conflict that drags on, a sense of being abandoned by a loved one, a child with health problems, or a rebuilding that has got out of hand – in time it will all pass, or at least my current state of suffering about it will change.

Practicing *equanimity* with the good and bad things that will inevitably happen in our own and our children's lives helps us to lessen our suffering and cultivate mindful parenting. Equanimity comes from the Latin *aequanimitas*, and means to have emotional stability even in times of stress. To be equanimous is to welcome all experiences, good and bad. So we should try to experience 'negative' emotions attentively, even at a physical level, rather than pushing them away or trying to numb them.

There are many ways in which humans try to avoid negative emotions – for example by misusing alcohol or food, by working hard, or by constantly being around other people. Welcoming negative feelings means seeing things just as they are, and accepting instead of resisting them, and we can practice it across all aspects of our lives, not just in our parenting. Acceptance doesn't mean passively shrugging our shoulders, but actively moving towards our feelings in order to experience and engage with the full spectrum of human emotion. The paradox is that only when we accept and let go do we acquire the power to change things.

As a mindful parenting trainer in a youth mental health care context, I often see parents with a child who has been diagnosed with a psychological condition. This could be anything from autism to an anxiety disorder, or from depression to an addiction. Mindful parenting is also taught in medical contexts, for parents of children with conditions such as cancer and chronic pain. All these difficulties can be assessed on a scale of how temporary or permanent they are likely to be. When parents are first confronted with their child's diagnosis, there may be no reliable information as to how changeable the issue is and what their situation may be like in five or ten years' time. This unpredictability and hope of a possible cure makes mourning the present situation complex: should they spend time accepting what is lost, or devote all their energies to trying to fix the problem?

In these situations, and even if the parents don't try to avoid their own negative emotions, the five stages of grief as described by Elisabeth Kübler-Ross[4] – denial, anger, bargaining, depression and acceptance – will be experienced multiple times as the child's condition changes. Other emotions, such as fear and shame, can also come up during this time, as well as guilt over whether the condition could have been avoided and survivor's guilt because the parents don't have the condition themselves (see Chapter 8). The ability to simply 'be' with this full spectrum of intense emotions, to sit on a cushion or couch and say *You can all come, I'm ready* is the part of mindful parenting that requires the most care. Yet it's well worth the effort, for it leads ultimately to the acceptance that is required to perceive and build on the unique needs and abilities of the individual child.

A parent in a mindful parenting group told me that she had found a lump in her breast, and that her mother had previously had breast cancer. When she called her mother to share the news, her mother reacted by saying, '*Oh no, I really can't deal with this on top of everything else right now!*'. Now, it's understandable of course that the news caused a flood of emotions in her mother; less clear is why, instead of attempting to manage these, the mother allowed herself to react in a way that was clumsy at best. If she had instead said, '*Darling, I need to let this sink in for half an hour, then I'll call you back*', and had sat down and told herself, '*It's alright, let me feel it*', then maybe things would have been different. Maybe she'd have realized how hard it was to see her daughter suffer, and how the news had caused her to relive emotions of fear, shame and powerlessness over her own cancer experience. By welcoming and accepting these feelings, she might have found something meaningful to share with her daughter, so that her daughter felt that her suffering was noticed and that her mother was there to support her.

Parental experiential avoidance can take place on two levels. Let's now look at a simpler example than a serious physical or psychological condition. Imagine that your young son gets up yet again because he can't sleep. He feels miserable, and worries that because he can't sleep he'll feel really tired again tomorrow. The first level of parental experiential avoidance is simply that you don't want your child to toss and turn in bed, worry about things or be tired during school. You want him to be happy, cheerful and fit. Ideally you'd put him to sleep with a magic wand, thereby laying all these negative feelings immediately to rest.

The second level of avoidance is the emotional impact on you as a parent. This might be stress and irritation because you still have work to finish and keep being distracted, disappointment because your child can't sleep as easily as other children (or at least as easily as you think they do), or exhaustion because you've had a hectic day and need time for yourself. It's also likely to involve a degree of worry about the wider consequences of your child's problem – such as feelings of guilt that he won't be able to concentrate at school, shame that the teacher will think you don't send your son to bed at an appropriate time, misery because you feel you're a bad parent, or anger at the medical professionals who don't take the problem seriously and leave you to deal with it on your own.

As a parent, you have a natural tendency to avoid your child's negative emotions and the negative emotions you experience yourself as a result of his problem. This can influence how you react: perhaps you'll angrily send him back to bed, or give up your plans for the night to sleep in the bed with him so that he falls asleep immediately. But what would happen if you took the time to sit down and really focus on how you felt about your child's inability to sleep or stay in bed?

What if you took a breathing space every time he got up – feeling your body and your breathing, and becoming aware of all the thoughts, feelings and worries that arose whenever he left his bed? What if you told yourself, 'It's alright, let me feel it!'. This is the beginning of accepting that your child feels the things he feels, and you feel the things you feel – and this acceptance will create the space needed to make a considered decision about how best to address the problem.

Whatever kind of behaviour or personality trait your child may have that troubles you – being unable to sleep, temper tantrums if they don't get what they want, refusal to eat during meals, spending all their time on the computer, never cleaning up after themselves, not doing their homework or anything else – try to become aware of your own emotional and physical reaction whenever this behaviour or trait shows itself. Observe closely what happens. What do you try to fight against? What don't you allow yourself to feel? Move your attention towards those feelings and sensations instead of pushing them away. Take a breathing pause. Give yourself compassion if you'd like. Think about Reinhold Niebuhr's serenity prayer:

'Grant me the serenity to accept the things I cannot change, the courage to change the things I can, and the wisdom to know the difference.'[5]

Your starting point for dealing with problematic behaviour, even changeable behaviour, must always be to accept the current state of events, i.e. how things are, now. Thich Nhat Hanh calls this beautifully *'The suchness of things'*. If you get home after a long day at work and find that the house you left tidy is one big mess, don't act immediately. Instead, sit down amid the chaos, look around, take everything in, and notice what happens to you on the inside. What do you feel? What's going on in your body? What action impulses do you notice? See the house exactly for what it is now. Tell yourself *'Let me feel this'*. Only then, when you're aware of the situation and your own emotional reaction, choose what to do. Whether that happens to be cleaning up, telling everyone else to clean up, leaving the mess where it is or even displaying a measured level of conscious anger, it's now a conscious choice based on full knowledge of the situation and your own state of mind.

Sometimes parents are faced with much more intense and serious situations that they must learn to accept. Perhaps their child has a degenerative disease, is a danger to others and needs to be treated in a secure facility, is suicidal, or is the innocent victim of a terrorist attack. These are all real things that have happened to the real parents of real children, and those parents had to learn to accept them. In your meditations you may choose to take these parents into your thoughts, and to wish them strength, resolution and peace.

Exercises

Exercise 9.1: Equanimity
Practice equanimity towards the weather. When you leave the house tomorrow look at the sky, feel the temperature and humidity of the air, and notice the effect of the sun or rain – all with equanimity. What sensations

are produced by the wind on your face, the rain on your cheeks, the sun on your skin? Watch the clouds move and the trees sway. Also be aware of your physical posture: if you find that you shrink into yourself whenever it's cold or rainy, open up! Accept and welcome the rain and cold, just as you would do on a warm sunny day.

Practice this same equanimity towards the moods and behaviours of your child. If your child cries, throws a tantrum, or is bad tempered, observe them with full attention, welcome their current emotional state, and notice its effect on you without judgment. Say to yourself: '*This too will pass*'. Cultivate the same equanimity when your child is in a happy mood – observe how they look and behave, and how it affects you. Say '*Thank you*' gently and kindly to yourself. Be grateful that you are experiencing this happiness, knowing that it too will pass.

Exercise 9.2: Sitting with a difficulty (audio track 8)

This can be a tough meditation in which you deliberately focus on a difficult situation or difficult feelings in order to achieve resolution and compassion. You can choose a situation or feeling that isn't too difficult to begin with, or if you don't feel up to an intense session – sometimes coming home tired and seeing that the children haven't emptied the dishwasher is hard enough! As you gain experience, try more difficult feelings and situations. Repeat the exercise every day this week. You can use audio track 8 or the text below; if you choose the text, set an alarm to end your meditation after ten minutes.

Sit in the meditation position. Take time to feel how you're sitting, here in this place at this moment – where your body makes contact with different surfaces, how your breath flows in and out of your body, and how you are. When you're settled, allow a parenting situation to arise in your mind where you felt stress or other negative feelings. For example a disobeyed request, a recent tantrum or a teacher wanting to see you because of your child's poor behaviour in school.

Imagine the situation as vividly as possible by asking yourself the following questions:

- Where was I?
- Who else was there?
- What happened?
- What did the other person (or people) say?
- What did I do or say?

Then ask yourself:

- How did I feel in that situation?
- What happened in my body?
- What emotions did I feel?

Now bring your attention back to your body, sitting here in the present. What do you notice? Any tension or other sensation? Feel in detail what happens in your body. Focus your attention on it. Say to yourself: '*It's ok, let me feel it!*' Move even closer to these bodily feelings – let your attention be there, without judgment. If you feel tension or discomfort, breathe into and out of this tension and discomfort. Whenever you notice your attention wandering away from the feelings and sensations, bring it back.

If the exercise becomes overwhelming, you can always return to feeling the contact of your body or the rhythm of your breath. When you feel settled again, redirect your attention to the tense or uncomfortable feeling. You can also choose to give yourself compassion while sitting with a difficulty. Say something like: '*I'm having a hard time*', or '*Poor* [your name], *it isn't easy to be a good parent*'. Put your hands on your heart if you wish, or embrace yourself.

It helps to repeat this practice, with the same or different parenting situations.

Exercise 9.3: Your child's worst behaviour as a meditation bell

Think about which of your child's behaviours disturbs you the most. Perhaps he keeps getting out of bed when you're longing for time to yourself, reacts badly to not getting his own way, doesn't brush his teeth well enough or oversleeps in the morning. Narrow it down to a single one – it should be something that happens regularly so that the practice is effective – and write the behaviour down.

Now, for the next week, use this behaviour as your personal meditation bell. Whenever the behaviour occurs, immediately take a three minute breathing space before choosing how or whether to respond. Make notes about what you learn by doing this. You may discover feelings and thoughts underlying what troubles you about this behaviour, or find that the breathing space consistently changes your usual response. You may even find that your child's behaviour changes with you. Be open to whatever comes out of this practice!

References

1   Rogers, C.R. (1995). *A way of being*. New York: Mariner Books.

2   Murray, L., Hentges, F., Hill, J., Karpf, J., Mistry, B., Kreutz, M., ... & Goodacre, T. (2008). The effect of cleft lip and palate, and the timing of lip repair on mother-infant interactions and infant development. *Journal of Child Psychology and Psychiatry*, **49**, 115-123.

3   Cheron, D. M., Ehrenreich, J. T., & Pincus, D. B. (2009). Assessment of parental experiential avoidance in a clinical sample of children with anxiety disorders. *Child Psychiatry and Human Development*, **40**, 383-403.

4   Kübler-Ross, E., & Kessler, D. (2014). *On grief and grieving: Finding the meaning of grief through the five stages of loss*. New York: Simon and Schuster.

5   Shapiro, F.R. (2014). 'Who Wrote the Serenity Prayer?', *The Chronicle Review*, April 28.

Chapter 10:
Schemas: Re-experiencing your own childhood

'In every real human, a child is hidden that wants to play.'
Friedrich Nietsche

Having and raising children (and grandchildren) is one of the most emotionally enriching journeys that we can experience in our lives. As our children grow up, so we relive our own childhood. When we help them build a sandcastle, defying the oncoming tide, we share the physical delight of sun, beach and water – the delight of packing wet sand into walls and sprinkling dry powdery sand on the tops of towers, and  the beauty of shells to decorate the castle. We share in the pride of creating the biggest, tallest and most impregnable structure possible, and we feel our own smallness when the force of the water tears it down nonetheless.

While we're doing this, the time (though never the tide…) stops – we're fully present in this moment, at one with our child. We also re-experience something of our own youth, because we connect with the child within us that wants to play. It is this double experience – delighting in our child as well as reconnecting with our own inner child – that gives parenting its unique emotional load.[1]

As well as our experiences of being a child, our experiences of being parented or otherwise cared for are also re-experienced when we become parents. When my first child was born, I was struck by the enormous responsibility that would last for the rest of my life. Suddenly I felt humility and deep respect for my own parents, who had taken on this responsibility for no less than five children. What an immense task, what courage, what dedication, what belief in life! Finally, as an insecure young parent, I began to understand the wisdom of the commandment: *'Honour thy father and mother'*.

During that first week as a mother I wrote my parents a long letter, in which I looked back on fond memories of my own childhood, thanking them for everything they'd done and all they meant to me. In my letter I connected myself with them – I was now one of them, a fellow parent. I voiced the hope that what I had learned from them I would pass on to my son. When my father died suddenly ten years later, I found this same letter under the writing pad of his desk – the place where he always sat and worked. How often did he re-read it, and how had it affected him? I will never know, but I hope that he felt the deep and sincere respect for him and my mother that I experienced at that time as a new parent.

While pregnant I had started to knit fanatically and sew self-designed dresses for the baby, creating sheets with my own embroidery patterns for the baby's bed and even making tiny shoes. These were handicrafts I'd learned from my mother during the endless happy hours of my childhood, but I hadn't done such things for years as a busy scientist and psychotherapist. Only now, writing this, do I realize that this wasn't just a nesting urge – I was also re-experiencing my youth in order to prepare for my role as a parent. It was the 13th century Zen master Dogen Zenji who said that when our child is born, we ourselves become a child[2]. How right he was.

Re-experiencing positive aspects of our youth and our relationship with our mothers and fathers when we ourselves become parents is an enjoyable experience; however many of us will re-experience not only positive but also negative aspects of how we were brought up. And despite our best efforts to pass on only positive aspects, sometimes we'll unintentionally also pass on negative aspects – or try so hard not to pass them on that we create new problems. For instance: the mother who felt neglected as a child because her parents were busy running a hotel is now so very available that she neglects herself and spoils her children; the father who was physically punished by his parents and teachers tries so hard not to lose his temper that he laughs when his children misbehave, thereby appearing not to take himself or his job as a parent seriously. By making a conscious effort to fully re-experience aspects of our upbringing, and to pass on positive aspects in a measured way, we can not only enrich our parenting but also enjoy it more.

Schema therapy, developed by psychologist Jeffrey Young[3,4], can be helpful in disentangling the jumble of memories and childhood events that are re-experienced during parenting. Schemas are internal mental representations of our past relationships with important attachment figures, such as our parents. Examples of such representations might be: '*if I cry, I'll be fed*', '*if I'm in pain, I'll be comforted*', '*if I get angry, I'll get a smack*', and '*if I break a rule, I'll be punished*'. However, schemas are far more than simple 'if-then' relationships; they also involve complex emotional and physical experiences and behaviour.

For example, *'if I get angry, I'll get a smack'* is bound up with emotions of anger and fear, physiological responses of stress and pain, and behaviors of expressing anger, avoiding a smack or withdrawing after a smack. Schemas are experienced whole – we experience the associated emotions, bodily feelings, thoughts and impulses all at once. Schemas are helpful to us in organizing reality so as to predict new situations; however they also generalize reality. So, for some people, the mental association *'if I'm angry, I'll get a smack'* may become generalized not just to *'if I'm angry, I may experience fear and withdrawal'* but to *'if I'm angry, I'll be rejected'*. A person who internalizes this schema may come to fear the consequences of expressing any anger, and may therefore repress all anger in order to avoid such consequences. We aren't born to please, we are made so.

Schemas inform how we view and experience relationships, how we behave in relationships, and how we choose new relationships. According to Young, there are adaptive (helpful/constructive) and maladaptive (toxic/self-defeating) schemas. The maladaptive schemas are likely to have been adaptive in certain past contexts. For example, the schema 'if I'm angry, I will be rejected' may have been adaptive for a child growing up in an environment where anger was often met with physical punishment. When, as an adult, that child seeks to live with a loving partner, however, the schema becomes maladaptive. So the adaptive or maladaptive properties of schemas can vary by context and relationship.

Schemas also tend to be self-perpetuating. We confirm them by selective perception, selective interpretation, selective memory, avoidance and repetition. For example, someone with the schema *'if I'm angry, I'll be rejected'* will tend to notice and remember situations in which anger leads to rejection. They will also remember situations in which anger caused rejection better than they remember situations in which it didn't, and interpret neutral or ambiguous responses to anger as rejection. Such individuals are likely to repress anger for as long as they can, but tend eventually to explode in a manner that makes rejection inevitable. In the worst cases, they may even choose an abusive partner who confirms the schema.

As parents, we can transmit maladaptive schemas born of the relationships we had with our caregivers via the relationships we have with our own children. These maladaptive schemas are activated by certain events. A mother's *'fear of abandonment'* schema might for example be triggered if her child tries to assert independence and screams in anger, '*I want a different mum!*' If the mother is divorced and the child screams that his/her stepmother is much nicer than her, then the schema will be triggered even more intensely. She will feel vulnerable and afraid, think that her child will leave her forever, and do everything in her power to prevent the supposed abandonment – for example spoiling the child, talking negatively about the stepmother, or even beginning formal custody proceedings.

Schemas can be viewed as our weak spots. They aren't always active, but when triggered they can change our whole way of thinking, feeling and acting. Young calls the way in which we are thinking, feeling and acting at any given moment a *mode*. Kathleen Restifo and I[1] argued that when parents are emotionally triggered by their children, they automatically and unconsciously slip into certain modes.

Suppose a father, reprimanding his child, points at the child with a reproachful finger. He thinks he is acting from what Young calls the 'healthy adult mode' (of which more later). But if he has been emotionally triggered by something, it may be that he is also responding from a different mode – either a 'child mode' or an 'internalized parent mode' – based on what he himself experienced as a child with his own parents or other significant attachment figures.

Let's first imagine that a 'child mode' is active. Through his interactions with his child, the father will re-experience himself as a child interacting with his own parents, and will re-experience how he felt when his parents reprimanded him for doing something wrong. Young distinguished three separate child modes (although there can be more). The 'vulnerable child' mode involves a child that was rejected, abandoned or perhaps even neglected or abused. The 'angry child' mode involves a child who is angry about unfulfilled needs and expresses this in an entitled, manipulative and egocentric way. Finally, the 'impulsive child' wears emotions on his sleeve, acts based on immediate desires, and follows his natural instinct from moment to moment without considering the consequences.

Alternatively, it may be the case that a 'maladaptive parent mode' is active. Through his interactions with his child, the father will again re-experience his interactions with his own parents – but this time from his parents' perspective, which he has internalized. Young distinguished two maladaptive parent modes, but again there can be more. The 'punitive parent' (punishing parent) criticizes and punishes the child in a harsh and unforgiving way for being 'naughty' (although the perceived 'naughtiness' is only showing normal needs that the father himself was not permitted by his parents to express), while the 'demanding parent' uses coercion, pressure and rigid organization to continually push the child to meet excessively high standards, and feels that it is wrong to express feelings or act spontaneously.

The unique emotional load of parenting (feeling and experiencing what our child feels and experiences, while at the same time re-experiencing our own childhood and how we ourselves were parented) amplifies our emotions – the good and the bad. So contact with our children increases our pleasure and happiness, but it can also strengthen feelings of anger, frustration, worry, fear and guilt. When strong emotions are triggered by an interaction with our child, it is very likely that we will respond from a child or internalized parent mode. Since modes describe the ways in which we think, feel and act at any given moment, it is possible for different modes to be active all at once or one after another at high speed.

Here is an example of a mother from one of my mindful parenting groups. The mother has a young daughter with autism; the daughter is very sensitive to pain, and screams when her mother brushes her hair in the morning. This makes the mother stressed and angry, causing her to brush even harder – which causes her daughter to scream even louder. This triggers feelings of despair in the mother – she feels she is a bad parent who doesn't look after her daughter well. By the time the school bus arrives, both mother and daughter are emotionally exhausted.

I asked the mother whether anything in this interaction reminded her of her own upbringing, or of her interactions with her own parents. She recalled that as a child she had to do everything herself, as her father had autism and her mother was always busy with her autistic brother who often misbehaved. She felt she had no space to be angry or difficult, because her mother couldn't handle any more problems. This caused her to feel jealous of her brother for monopolizing her mother's attention – and some of that same jealousy had now been attached to her daughter, because of the constant and unrequited attention she received from a mother who had herself received very little attention as a child.

I then asked whether she recognized any of the child or internalized parent modes in her interactions with her daughter. She immediately recognized the 'angry child' mode – the child who is angry to have received no attention while her brother did, and who now receives no attention from her own daughter. I asked if she recognized any other modes. After some thought, she recognized the 'demanding parent' mode – the child who was expected by her parents to do everything herself, who now expects to do everything herself for her daughter, and who feels she is a bad mother when the smallest thing goes wrong. Suddenly, she remembered that when she was young her mother once cut her hair against her will because she didn't brush it enough. This memory unlocked the 'punitive parent' mode – the mother who now brushes her daughter's hair too hard.

Last of all, I asked what the mother's angry child and/or demanding and punitive parents might need from her 'healthy adult' mode. The healthy adult is at the core of schema therapy – it's our compassionate, nurturing, wise and assertive side who can recognize limits, set priorities and experience self-worth. If it is strong enough, the healthy adult mode can placate and subdue all the maladaptive modes. The mother replied that her healthy adult wanted to comfort the angry child because her parents forgot her, and to tell her that she was justified in being angry with her parents and jealous of her brother. She said that in future she wouldn't forget her inner angry child, and would be mindful of what she needed. After brushing her daughter's hair, she would take a moment to give herself compassion by putting her hands on her heart and saying to herself: '*It's hard to raise my daughter*'. Her final comment, tellingly, was that perhaps it was time she taught her daughter how to brush her own hair.

So, how can schema modes help in practical ways with your life as a busy parent? It's critical to realize that whenever strong emotions are triggered in contact with your child, and you automatically react in ways that you are later unhappy with, you have probably experienced either a 'fight or flight' response (see Chapter 1), or one of your maladaptive schema modes. In such a triggered state the first step is always to take a breathing space and/or give yourself compassion. Next, you can follow the 'recognizing schema modes' practice below in order to gain insight into what maladaptive modes might have been triggered, and to understand how you can take care of them from your healthy adult mode.

By taking care of the child and internalized parent modes within you, you can improve your parenting and the care you provide for your child. In my mindful parenting groups I see parents suddenly recognize how, when their child has a tantrum, they get worked up too (angry child mode). This is often a moment of epiphany. The classic learning process has four stages: unconscious incompetence (when a learner is unaware that a knowledge gap exists), conscious incompetence (when the lack of knowledge is recognized and learning can begin), conscious competence (when applying the knowledge requires effort) and unconscious competence (when it has become second nature). When parents recognize that they have an angry child mode, they instantly move from unconscious incompetence to conscious incompetence and are thus ready to begin improving themselves and their parenting skills.

That we must take particularly good care of ourselves when we are angry is elegantly illustrated by Thich Nhat Hanh[5]:

'Anger is like a howling baby, suffering and crying. The baby needs his mother to embrace him. You are the mother for your baby, your anger. The moment you begin to practice breathing mindfully in and out, you have the energy of a mother, to cradle and embrace the baby. Just embracing your anger, just breathing in and breathing out, that is good enough. The baby will feel relief right away... Embrace your anger with much tenderness. Your anger is not your enemy, your anger is your baby.'

Exercises

Exercise 10.1: Recognizing schema modes

Describe a parent-child interaction in which you felt intense emotions triggered by the behaviour of your child, and after which you were unhappy about your behaviour (overreactive parenting). Consider whether this situation reminds you in any way of your own upbringing, and see if you can identify any child or internalized parent modes. If so, think about how you can take care of them. Here's an example:

Trigger
■ Describe the stressful interaction

The children make a lot of noise – our neighbour below gets very angry about this, but my husband ignores it or even seems to encourage it.

Behaviour pattern
■ Describe your overreactive parenting

I keep warning them, but nobody listens to me

Own history
■ Does the situation reminds you of anything from your own upbringing?

I always had to be silent at home because my mother had a long-term illness. This also meant I had lots of responsibilities and had to look after myself.

Schema modes
■ Describe the 'angry, vulnerable or impulsive child' modes, and/or the 'demanding or punitive internalized parent' modes that are at work

A vulnerable child that worried about her mother, spent a lot of time alone, and did her very best but got little recognition or attention.

What do I need?
■ How can I take care of my child and/or internalized parent modes?

Although I feel alone, I am not – my husband can help me resolve the issue with the neighbour. I will ask him to support me because I feel vulnerable.

Exercise 10.2: Mindfulness day within the family

Being mindful for a whole day, as best you can in the midst of your normal family life, is a practice that can help you integrate mindfulness into your everyday routine and your role as a parent.

A mindful day has parallels with the Jewish Sabbath – something I experienced when I lived with my family in London, and Jewish friends invited us over. They'd prepared everything the evening before, as work is forbidden on the Sabbath. Our friends and their children were out in the garden; there was conversation, playing in the grass, a board game, football. Both parents were completely relaxed and open. Everyone enjoyed the delicious food that was set out. No TV, no phones, no newspaper, no computer. If the children wanted to visit friends, they couldn't call them and had to walk there, because mechanical transport was not allowed. There was an atmosphere of peace, connectedness, warmth and endless time. We felt so welcome and surprised by this calm in the midst of London turmoil that we dropped other plans and stayed for the whole day.

Choose a day when you'll be around your family, but don't have obligations or appointments – a weekend day is often best. Tell your partner in advance that you're going to have a mindfulness day, and explain briefly how the day will work and the accommodations that you'll need from your partner and family. How much you explain in advance to your children will depend on their ages.

On your mindfulness day, separate yourself from external distractions such as television, recorded music (playing instruments yourself or listening to the family make music is fine), newspapers, post, email, Internet and phone. Make sure that in the rooms you'll be in there is no computer, TV or music, and no phones. Also avoid reading, or any work that you might usually do in a home office. Don't drink alcohol, and limit your consumption of caffeinated drinks like tea and coffee.

Whatever you do during this day, do it mindfully. If it's housework, approach it with the dedication of a monk – completely focused on the task in hand (cleaning, peeling potatoes, washing up or whatever it might be) without rushing to get it done as soon as possible. Commit yourself fully to the activity you're engaged in, no matter how mundane, without questioning it or asking why someone else isn't doing it instead.

Create a schedule for your day (write it down in your notebook), that includes periods of meditation or yoga, periods of mindful eating and drinking, periods of work meditation (non-stressful, repetitive work such as cleaning, gardening or ironing), periods of mindful time and/or activities with the children, and periods of mindful time and/or activities with your partner. For example:

07.00	Morning sitting meditation
07.45	Make breakfast mindfully
08.00	Drink a cup of tea mindfully before waking the family
08.15	Wake family mindfully (first taking a moment to watch how they sleep)
08.30	Eat breakfast mindfully, with mindful speaking and listening
09.30	Go for an hour-long walk, alone or with a family member; if the latter then practice mindful speaking and listening and observe periods of silence
10.30	Mindful playing, being, or talking with the children
11.00	Mindful working in the garden
12.30	Drink a cup of coffee mindfully
12.45	Prepare lunch mindfully
13.15	Eat lunch mindfully
14.15	Sleep, rest or meditate
15.00	Mindful playing, being, or talking with the children
15.30	Mindful yoga or other refreshing physical activity e.g. swimming
16.15	Mindful reading of a spiritual book, drawing, or making music
17.30	Prepare dinner mindfully, give family members dinner tasks mindfully
18.30	Dinner – eat, speak and listen mindfully
20.00	Mindful walking or playing of a game with the family
21.00	Putting the children to bed mindfully (or asking partner to do this)
21.30	Meditation
22.15	Bed

References

1   Bögels, S. M., & Restifo, K. (2014). *Mindful parenting: A guide for mental health practitioners*. New York: Springer, Norton.

2   Tanahashi, K. (1995). *Moon in a dewdrop. Writings of Zen Master Dogen*. New York: New Point Press.

3   Young, J.E., Klosko, J.S. & Weishaar, M.E. (2006). *Schema therapy: A Practitioner's guide*. New York: Guilford Press.

4   Young, J.E. & Klosko, J.S. (1994). *Reinventing your life: The breakthrough program to end negative behavior and feel great again: How top break free from negative life patterns*. New York: Plume.

5   Nhat Hanh, T. (2001). *Anger: Wisdom for cooling the flame*. New York: Riverhead Books.

Chapter 11:
Lifelong parenting

'Perfect love sometimes does not come until the first grandchild.'
Gore Vidal

Picture a scene. I'm lying back in my dentist's chair, my mouth full of equipment. My dentist is a friendly, capable professional, and I like and trust her. She begins chatting:

'I've googled you… about this mindful parenting thing. I wish I'd known about it when my daughter was young. I remember when she was a baby, after a day of work in my practice, I sometimes found it hard to go back to her. I would postpone it by doing more admin, or calling one more patient. My work was very predictable – the exact opposite of motherhood. Now she's a young adult, it's too late…'

'No!' I would have shouted, but for all the equipment stuffed into my mouth. In fact it's never too late to notice your parenting, or to interact with your child with renewed attention. After all, you'll be a parent for the rest of your life (and beyond).

When I first began providing mindful parenting courses to parents of children with severe behavioural problems[1] (some of whom had a criminal record, were no longer allowed in school, abused drugs or had potentially dangerous family relationships), many parents spoke to me afterwards. Often they would sigh and say, *'I wish I'd done this course earlier – maybe I could have stopped things from getting so out of hand'*. That's why we adapted the course to parents of younger children with behaviour problems, and why we now provide mindful parenting courses for parents with babies[2] and pregnant couples[3].

Eva Potharst, a mindful parenting trainer and infant mental health specialist, has developed a course called 'Being Mindful with Your Baby' in which she meditates with groups of new mothers. The mothers attend the course with their babies, and practice bringing their full attention onto the infant (what does it need, what is it experiencing, what does it want to express?) and then back to themselves (what do I need, what am I experiencing, how am I doing?). By doing so they learn to find a balance between attention for their children and attention for themselves.

Irene Veringa, a midwife and obstetrician who is now a mindful parenting trainer, offers 'Mindfulness Based Childbirth and Parenting' (MBCP) courses to anxious pregnant women and their partners. The expectant mothers may be fearful about pregnancy, the birth itself or their future role as parents. MBCP helps them to practice mindful parenting from the very first moments of their maternal journey by using here-and-now, non-judgmental attention to perceive the changes that will occur in their bodies through pregnancy, childbirth and beyond – and to then bring this same level of conscious attention to their developing child, their relationship with it, and their changing relationship with their partner.

Mindful parenting, then, can begin long before a baby is even born. And happily, at the other extreme, it's never too late for us to learn. Relationships continue developing throughout our lives, and in every phase of parenting and grandparenting we can practice giving conscious, non-judgmental attention to our children and grandchildren, and working on our relationships with them. Though my own children are now grown adults, I continually discover new aspects of mindful parenting. Sometimes I worry about how they are, especially if they're coping with setbacks like illness, unemployment or the end of a relationship. I tend to try to take care of them again in times like this, or to interfere with their lives – telling them what they should do (as if I know that). Of course, what they really need is for me to trust their choices and their assessments of risk and reward, but it isn't always easy. I know that if I see them as whole individual beings, and let go of them in love, then they'll come back to me if they need my attention, support and sometimes even advice (which is very different from me giving it out unasked).

I've made peace with what I need in order to let them go. I remember that when my son, then aged just 17, made a long trip through India (something I always wanted to do but never found the courage to), he suggested mailing us once a week with a travel report. That made it so much easier for me to trust that he was safe, with the bonus that I got to co-experience some of his travel! Children need space to make mistakes and learn from them. After that, we can only hope that they trust us to provide comfort and support if they feel in need of it – but they'll only do so if they know we won't say: '*I told you so*'.

Thich Nhat Hanh[4], referring to the 'Right View' that is a cornerstone of Buddhism (and means, in simple terms, having a clear understanding of reality and insight concerning the consequences of our actions), says:

> *'Sometimes we see our children doing things that we know will cause them to suffer in the future, but when we try to tell them, they won't listen. All we can do is to stimulate the seeds of Right View in them, and then later, in a difficult moment, they may benefit from our guidance. We cannot explain an orange to someone who has never tasted one. No matter how well we describe it, we cannot give someone else the direct experience. He has to taste it for himself. As soon as we say a single word, he is already caught. Right View cannot be described. We can only point in the correct direction. Right View cannot even be transmitted by a teacher. A teacher can help us identify the seed of Right View that is already in our garden, and help us have the confidence to practice, to entrust that seed to the soil of our daily life. But we are the gardener. We have to learn how to water the wholesome seeds that are in us so they will bloom into the flowers of Right View. The instrument for watering wholesome seeds is mindful living — mindful breathing, mindful walking, living each moment of our day in mindfulness.'*

Not only is it never too late to practice mindful parenting, it is also never possible to be a 'finished' mindful parent – the journey has no endpoint. It's about doing as well as you possibly can, each and every day. If I find that I'm disappointed with any aspect of an interaction with my children, that's fine. I'll sit with it, look at it with attention to them, the interaction and myself, give myself compassion, and connect myself to other parents who also make mistakes. I'll then revisit the interaction, and finally draw lessons from it so that I can do better next time.

And best of all, each morning I get to start mindful parenting all over again!

Exercises

Exercise 11.1: Your mindful parenting plan

Make a plan for how you'll build mindfulness and mindful parenting into your life, starting with a finite period of time. If you've read through this book and now want to use it as a self-help course, focus on one chapter per week and do the relevant exercises. That will be a plan of 11 weeks. Include an idea of how often you plan to meditate each week, which meditations you'll try, where you'll sit, when and for how long. The more concrete and specific your plan, the greater the chance that you'll see it through to completion successfully.

Be sure to include mindful parenting practices in your plan – such as activities shared with your child with full attention, or a mindful family nature walk. You might also want to consider participating in a silent meditation retreat of one or more days, taking yoga lessons or joining a formal meditation group. Meditating regularly with other people can be very helpful for motivation, just like exercising, playing sports or trying to lose weight together.

Hang your plan somewhere prominent so you don't forget, and commit to it fully. At the end of the period, look back at how it went. Then ask yourself how you'd like to continue – for example by committing to mindfulness for the next year.

Exercise 11.2: Coming to the breath with kindness (audio track 9)

This is a short meditation to cultivate bringing kindness to yourself and those around you, like your children.

References

1. Bögels, S., Hoogstad, B., van Dun, L., de Schutter, S., & Restifo, K. (2008). Mindfulness training for adolescents with externalizing disorders and their parents. *Behavioural and Cognitive Psychotherapy*, **36**, 193-209.

2. Potharst, E. , Aktar, E., Rexwinkel, M., Rigterink, M., & Bögels, S.M. (2017). Mindful with your baby: Feasibility, acceptability, and effects of a mindful parenting group training for mothers and their babies in a mental health context. *Mindfulness*, **8**, 1236-1250.

3. Veringa, I. K., de Bruin, E. I., Bardacke, N., Duncan, L. G., van Steensel, F. J., Dirksen, C. D., & Bögels, S. M. (2016). 'I've changed my mind', Mindfulness-Based Childbirth and Parenting (MBCP) for pregnant women with a high level of fear of childbirth and their partners: Study protocol of the quasi-experimental controlled trial. *BMC Psychiatry*, **16**, 377.

4. Nhat Hanh, T. (2010). *The heart of Buddha's teachings: Transforming suffering into peace, love and liberation*. London: Rider.

Appendix

11 everyday rules for mindful parenting

1. Remember the words of the airline stewardess: put on your own mask before fitting your child's. If you don't take care of yourself, how can you possibly expect to take care of anyone else? If you ever experience feelings of guilt when making time to take care of your own needs, remember that you're ultimately doing it for the good of your child and your family.

2. Chose a personal meditation bell – your baby crying, your children fighting, arguing with your partner, the kitchen being left in a mess. Whenever the situation occurs, pause and take at least one breath mindfully – inhaling the whole way in, and exhaling the whole way out – before deciding what to do.

3. Take three mindful breaths when you wake each morning, before getting out of bed. Or spend one minute listening with full attention to all sounds, close by and far away. Can you hear your partner breathing, birds singing, your child waking? Or practice a one-minute seeing meditation, looking around your bedroom (or at your partner) as if this is the first time you've seen it.

4. Observe your child mindfully, with a beginner's mind. Watch as he or she wakes up, comes out of school, eats dinner, goes to bed and so on. See and enjoy the wonder of your child, just for a moment. If you wish, say in your head *'Namaste'* (which means *'I bow to you'* or *'I greet the divine in you'*).

5. In stressful interactions with your child or others, feel where your body makes contact with what you're sitting or standing on. Notice your breathing.

6. Listen mindfully to whatever your child has to say to you, and speak mindfully to your child. Breathe between your sentences.

7. Think of your child as your personal Zen master, sent from a higher authority to teach you everything you need to know about yourself, your child and the world around you. Remind yourself of this whenever you're experiencing difficulties with your child or your parenting.

8. When you pick up your child from school or nursery, walk the last few steps with full attention or stand still for a moment – aware of your body, your breath and the contact of the soles of your feet with the ground. Are you ready to be really present for this moment of reconnecting with your child?

9. Practice mindful housework, feeding your child mindfully, mindful shopping and so on. See if you can create more and more mindful moments each day.

10. Make mindfulness part of your daily routine – something you do whether you feel like it or not, just like showering or brushing your teeth. It doesn't matter whether you meditate for a minute or an hour; it's about spending time every day on your meditation cushion, and building up the routine.

And finally...

11. Remember that it's never too late to renew your intention to tread the path of mindfulness and mindful parenting. The next breath is always waiting for you, and so is the next interaction with your journey's guiding light – your child.

Further information

The chapters of this book are related to the eight sessions of the mindful parenting course from the book *Mindful Parenting: A guide for mental health practitioners* of Bögels, S.M. & Restifo, K. (2014). New York: Springer, Norton:

1. Attentive parenting (session 1)
2. Being your own parent (session 2)
3. Parenting stress (session 4)
4. Parental expectations and the true nature of the child (session 2)
5. Rupture and repair (session 6)
6. Parenting together in good and bad times (session 6)
7. Limit setting (session 5)
8. Guilt and shame (session 5)
9. Love makes blind (session 7)
10. Schemas (session 5)
11. A lifelong parenting (session 8 and follow-up session)

Some of the mindful parenting exercises described in this book are partially based on the exercises that have been previously described in *Mindful Parenting: A guide for mental health practitioners* of Bögels, S.M. & Restifo, K. (2014). New York: Springer, Norton.

The general mindfulness meditations described in this book and included in the audiotracks are based on the deep wisdom and work of meditation teachers and mindfulness program developers and researchers, especially from the Mindfulness-based Stress Reduction program of Jon Kabat-Zinn, and the Mindfulness-based Cognitive Therapy of Depression of Zindel Segal, Mark Williams and John Teasdale. A deep bow for their work, their wisdom, and for giving the world MBSR and MBCT. I have chosen not to reproduce their versions of the general meditations, especially because I wanted the practices for this book, given how busy parents are, to last for a maximum of 10 minutes. The recorded mindfulness practices are modified from the versions described in the books *Mindfulness: A practical guide to finding peace in a frantic world* by Williams, M., & Penman, D. (2011). London: Piatkus, and *The Mindful Way Through Depression. Freeing yourself from chronic unhappiness* by Williams, M., Teasdale, J., Segal, Z., & Kabat-Zinn, J. (2007). New York: Guilford Press. So readers who want to try out the original and somewhat longer versions of these meditations, please find them in these books and on their accompanying websites.

The meditations for this book are recorded by UK mindfulness teacher Trish Bartley, for more information on Trish see: http://trishbartley.co.uk/

The audio tracks can be downloaded from www.pavpub.com/mindful-parenting-resources and are as follows:

1. Sitting meditation: breath and body, 10 minutes
2. Body scan with self-compassion, 10 minutes
3. Sitting meditation with attention for sounds and thoughts, 10 minutes
4. Breathing space, 3 minutes
5. Walking meditation, 10 minutes
6. Choiceless awareness meditation, 10 minutes
7. Mindful movement, 10 minutes
8. Sitting with difficult feelings, 10 minutes
9. Coming to the breath with kindness, 7 minutes

If you want to further explore mindful parenting or mindfulness in general, group courses are offered at many mindfulness or health care centres.

A word of thanks

Leyla Perotti, next to being my daughter and my personal Buddha teacher, thank you for helping translating this book in English. Darren Reed from Pavilion Publishing, thank you for your personal touch in correcting the draft English version of the book and the support and guidance in publishing it. Trish Bartley, you are an amazing mindfulness teacher and I was so lucky that you were willing to provide the audio meditations for the book, a big thanks.

Mindfulness pioneers Chris Germer, Jon Kabat-Zinn, Nirbhay Singh, Lienhard Valentin, and Mark Williams, you have inspired and supported me in developing mindful parenting. I'm grateful for the dedication and fruitful collaboration in the clinical development and research of mindful parenting of my clinical and research colleagues Evin Aktar, Jeanine Baartmans, Ed de Bruin, Esther de Bruin, Eddie Brummelmans, Lisa Emerson, Anne Formsma, Joke Hellemans, Renee Meppelink, Eva Potharst, Anna Ridderinkhof, Rachel Vandermeulen and Irena Veringa.

Parents who participated in a mindful parenting course, you've been such an important source of inspiration, thanks for your trust. Professionals around the world who took a mindful parenting teacher training, I've learned so much from your openness as professional, parent and individual.

My parents, Joop and Nans: I benefit more and more from the special upbringing I received. My siblings, Paul, Gert, Corien and Cecile, you were part of my upbringing, thanks for your love and company, the endless playing and chatting, I still long for how we used to live together, but who knows, when we are old maybe we'll do that again! My children Thomas, Renate and Leyla, your lives give meaning to mine, it is a privilege to grow with you!

Susan Bögels
www.susanbogels.com

BV - #0073 - 211123 - C0 - 229/152/6 - PB - 9781912755769 - Matt Lamination